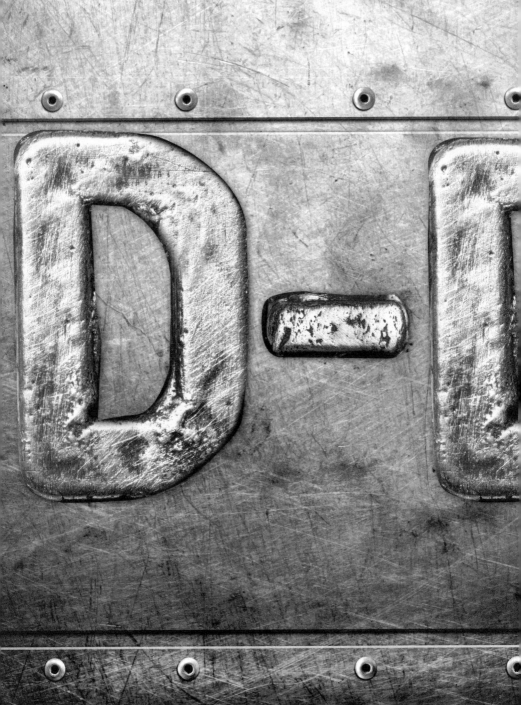

ADAPTED FROM **THE GUNS AT LAST LIGHT**

DAY

RICK ATKINSON

with KATE WATERS

HENRY HOLT AND COMPANY
NEW YORK

Henry Holt and Company, LLC
Publishers since 1866
175 Fifth Avenue
New York, New York 10010
mackids.com

Library of Congress Cataloging-in-Publication Data
Atkinson, Rick.
D-Day : adapted from The guns at last light / Rick Atkinson. — First edition.
pages   cm
Includes bibliographical references and index.
ISBN 978-1-62779-111-3 (hardcover) • ISBN 978-1-62779-112-0 (e-book)
1. World War, 1939–1945—Campaigns—France—Normandy—Juvenile literature.
I. Atkinson, Rick Guns at last light.   II. Title.
D756.5.N6A75 2014   940.54'21421—dc23   2014005162

First Edition—2014
Based on the book *The Guns at Last Light* by Rick Atkinson,
published by Henry Holt and Company, LLC.
Designed by April Ward
Maps by Gene Thorp
Printed in the United States of America by
R. R. Donnelley & Sons Company, Harrisonburg, Virginia

3   5   7   9   10   8   6   4   2

CONTENTS

MAP LEGEND

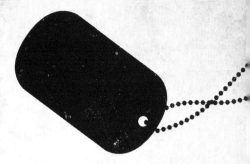

~~ River/stream

HIGHWAY

MAJOR ROAD

MINOR ROAD /TRAIL

RAILROAD

 Wooded

Swamp

Terrain

• City/town/village with urban area

✪ **Capital city**

■ Landmark

AXIS   ### ALLIED

   Front line

   Airborne drop

TYPE OF UNIT

   Infantry

   Airborne

   Glider

 UNITED STATES

UNITED KINGDOM

CANADA

GERMANY

GROUPS IN AN ARMY IN DECREASING SIZE

Army Group	400,000–1,000,000 (approx. personnel)	**Brigade**	4,500+
		Regiment	1,500+
Army	100,000+	**Battalion**	300–1,300
Corps	30,000+	**Company**	80-225
Division	7,500–15,000+		

ALLIED COUNTRIES AND CHAIN OF COMMAND ON JUNE 6, 1944–PARTIAL LIST

BELGIUM

- KING LEOPOLD III
- HUBERT PIERLOT, Prime Minister
- GENERAL VICTOR VAN STRYDONCK DE BURKEL, Commander of the Belgian forces in Great Britain and Chief of the Belgian Military Mission to Supreme Headquarters Allied Expeditionary Force (SHAEF)

BRITISH EMPIRE AND COMMONWEALTH

- KING GEORGE VI, King of the United Kingdom and Dominions of the British Commonwealth

AUSTRALIA

- JOHN CURTAIN, Prime Minister
- SIR THOMAS BLAMEY, (Field Marshal) Commander in Chief of the Australian military forces

CANADA

- WILLIAM LYON MACKENZIE KING, Prime Minister
- HARRY CRERAR, General and *de facto* commander of the Canadian military

UNITED KINGDOM OF GREAT BRITAIN AND NORTHERN IRELAND

- WINSTON CHURCHILL, Prime Minister
- ANDREW CUNNINGHAM, First Sea Lord, head of the Royal Navy

- CHARLES PORTAL, Chief of the Air Staff, head of the Royal Air Force
- BERNARD MONTGOMERY, 1st Viscount Montgomery of Alamein, Field Marshal in command of the 21st Army Group and all Allied ground forces during Operation OVERLORD
- HUGH DOWDING, 1st Baron Dowding, Air Chief Marshal RAF Fighter Command

REPUBLIC OF CHINA

- CHIANG KAI-SHEK, leader of the Nationalist Government of the Republic of China and Supreme Commander of the Chinese theater

FREE FRENCH FORCES

- CHARLES DE GAULLE, leader of the Free French, head of the French government in exile, and head of the French Army of Liberation
- MAJOR GENERAL JACQUES-PHILIPPE LECLERC, in command of Free French forces in France

POLISH GOVERNMENT IN EXILE

- WŁADYSŁAW RACZKIEWICZ, President of the Polish government in exile
- STANISŁAW MIKOŁAJCZYK, Prime Minister of the Polish government in exile
- KAZIMIERZ SOSNKOWSKI, Commander in Chief of the Polish Armed Forces

SOVIET UNION

- JOSEPH STALIN, General Secretary of the Communist Party, Premier of the Soviet Union
- GEORGY ZHUKOV, Field Marshal
- NIKOLAY GERASIMOVICH KUZNETSOV, Admiral of the Soviet Navy
- VYACHESLAV MOLOTOV, Foreign Minister

UNITED STATES OF AMERICA

- FRANKLIN D. ROOSEVELT, President
- GEORGE MARSHALL, General and Chief of Staff of the U.S. Army
- HENRY H. ARNOLD, Commanding General of the U.S. Army Air Forces

- **ERNEST KING**, Commander in Chief of the U.S. Fleet, Chief of Naval Operations, and Fleet Admiral
- **HENRY L. STIMSON**, Secretary of War

EUROPEAN FRONT

- **DWIGHT D. EISENHOWER**, Supreme Commander of the Allied forces in Europe
- **OMAR N. BRADLEY**, General of the U.S. Army
- **JACOB L. DEVERS**, Commander of the 6th Army Group in Europe
- **CARL ANDREW SPAATZ**, Commander of the Air Forces Combat Command
- **ROYAL E. INGERSOLL**, Commander in Chief of the U.S. Atlantic Fleet

AXIS COUNTRIES AND CHAIN OF COMMAND ON JUNE 6, 1944–PARTIAL LIST

THE THIRD REICH (NAZI GERMANY)

- **ADOLF HITLER**, Führer
- **HEINRICH HIMMLER**, Supreme Commander of the Home Army
- **HERMANN GÖRING**, Commander in Chief of the Luftwaffe, *Reichsmarschall* of the Greater German Reich
- **ALBERT SPEER**, German Minister of Armaments
- **WILHELM KEITEL**, General and Chief of the High Command of the German military
- **GERD VON RUNDSTEDT**, Field Marshal of the German Army
- **ERWIN ROMMEL**, in command of the German forces during the Battle of Normandy

EMPIRE OF JAPAN

- **HIROHITO**, Emperor, Commander of the Imperial General Headquarters
- **HIDEKI TOJO**, Prime Minister
- **MITSUMASA YONAI**, Minister of the Imperial Japanese Navy
- **OSAMI NAGANO**, Chief of Staff of the Imperial Japanese Navy
- **TOMOYUKI YAMASHITA**, Lieutenant General of the Imperial Japanese Army

ITALIAN SOCIAL REPUBLIC

- **BENITO MUSSOLINI**, Head of State
- **RODOLFO GRAZIANI**, Minister of Defense
- **GIOVANNI MESSE**, Commander of the Italian Expeditionary Corps in Russia

WORLD WAR II TIMELINE

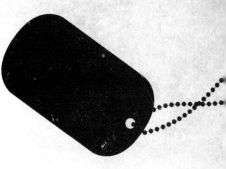

1939

MAY 22
Adolf Hitler of Germany signs a treaty with Italy's Benito Mussolini

AUGUST 23
Joseph Stalin of Russia and Adolf Hitler sign a pact vowing not to invade each other's countries

SEPTEMBER 1
Germany invades Poland

SEPTEMBER 3
Britain and France declare war on Germany

SEPTEMBER 10
The Parliament of Canada declares war on Germany

DECEMBER 18
First Canadian troops arrive in Europe

1940

MAY 9
Germany invades Denmark and Norway

MAY 10
Germany invades Holland, Belgium, and Luxembourg

MAY 15
Holland surrenders

JUNE 10
Italy declares war on Britain and France

JUNE 14
Germany invades Paris, and France surrenders to the Nazis

JUNE 28
Charles de Gaulle is recognized as the leader of the Free French

Forces, French troops who had escaped to Britain after the Nazis occupied France

JULY 10
The Battle of Britain between the RAF and the Luftwaffe begins in the skies over England

SEPTEMBER 7
The German Blitz against London begins

SEPTEMBER 13
Italian forces invade Egypt

SEPTEMBER 17
Hitler postpones invasion of Britain after losing air battle

OCTOBER 7
German troops enter Romania

OCTOBER 28
Italy invades Greece

1941

APRIL 27
German troops
occupy Athens

JUNE 1
The Nazi SS begin
mass murder of Jews
in eastern Poland

JUNE 22
Germans launch
massive invasion of
the Soviet Union

DECEMBER 7
The Japanese attack
the U.S. Navy base at
Pearl Harbor, Hawaii

DECEMBER 8
The U.S. Congress
declares war on Japan

DECEMBER 11
Germany and Italy
declare war on the U.S.
The U.S. Congress
declares war on
Germany and Italy

1942

JANUARY 26
U.S. troops arrive in
Europe

FEBRUARY 15
The British surrender
to Japanese forces in
Singapore

APRIL 1
Internment of U.S.
Japanese-American
citizens begins

JUNE 4–7
The U.S. wins decisive
Battle of Midway,
sinking four Japanese
aircraft carriers

JULY 6
Anne Frank and her
family go into hiding
in Amsterdam

AUGUST
Germany attacks
the Russian city of
Stalingrad

NOVEMBER 8
The U.S. invasion of
North Africa begins

1943

JANUARY 10
Soviets begin offensive
against Germans in
Stalingrad

JANUARY 23
U.S. troops take Tripoli
(now Libya)

FEBRUARY 1
Germans surrender
to Soviet forces in
Stalingrad

MAY
Allied troops
defeat the Germans
in North Africa

JULY 5
Germans launch the
largest tank battle
in history at Kursk,
Russia

JULY 9
Allied invasion of
Sicily, an island off
Italy, begins

JULY 25
Benito Mussolini is
arrested, ending the
Fascist regime in Italy

SEPTEMBER 8
Italy surrenders to the
Allies; Hitler rushes
troops to Italy

OCTOBER 13
Italy declares war on
Germany

NOVEMBER 1
U.S. Marines land on
the Japanese-occupied
Solomon Islands in the
Pacific Ocean

NOVEMBER 28

Roosevelt, Churchill, and Stalin meet in Yalta in Crimea to plan the final assault on and occupation of Germany

DECEMBER 1

Erwin Rommel becomes commander in chief of the German forces responsible for the defense of the Normandy coast

1944

JANUARY 17

Allies launch first attack against Germans in Italy

JANUARY 27

Soviet forces break the German 900-day siege of Leningrad, Russia, during which more than one million civilians died of starvation

FEBRUARY 20–25

German aircraft factories are bombed by U.S. and British air forces

MARCH 15

Germans launch offensive against India

APRIL 28

German E-boats attack Allied forces training for D-Day at Slapton Sands, England, killing nearly 700

JUNE 4

Allies liberate Rome, Italy, the first Axis capital to be freed when Canadians break the Hitler line south of the city

JUNE 6

D-Day

JULY 18

U.S. troops capture St.-Lô, France

JULY 21

U.S. Marines land on Japanese-occupied Guam in the Mariana Islands

JULY 29

Allies take Cherbourg, France

AUGUST 4

Anne Frank and her family are arrested

AUGUST 15

Allies launch the invasion of southern France

AUGUST 25

German troops in Paris surrender to the Allies

SEPTEMBER 3

The British liberate Brussels, the capital of Belgium

SEPTEMBER 17–22

Third Canadian Infantry division liberates French ports of Boulogne and Calais

OCTOBER 20

U.S. invasion of the Philippines begins

OCTOBER 25

First Japanese kamikaze attack on a U.S. ship occurs

DECEMBER 16

The Battle of the Bulge begins

1945

JANUARY 17

Soviet troops capture Warsaw, Poland

JANUARY 25

The Battle of the Bulge ends

JANUARY 26
Soviet troops liberate the Auschwitz death camp in Poland

FEBRUARY 19
U.S. Marines begin assault on the Japanese island of Iwo Jima

FEBRUARY 23
U.S. Marines raise the American flag on Mt. Suribachi, Iwo Jima

MARCH 7
U.S. troops cross into Germany on the Rhine River bridge at Remagen

MARCH 26
The battle for Iwo Jima ends

APRIL 1
U.S. troops land on the Japanese island of Okinawa

APRIL 11
U.S. troops liberate the Buchenwald concentration camp

APRIL 12
President Roosevelt dies suddenly; Harry Truman is sworn in as U.S. president

APRIL 15
British troops liberate the Bergen-Belsen camp, where Anne Frank and her sister had died of typhus one month earlier

APRIL 30
Hitler commits suicide as Soviet troops approach Berlin

MAY 7
General Eisenhower accepts Germany's unconditional surrender

MAY 8
Germany surrenders to Russia

JUNE 5
Allies divide Germany into four zones

AUGUST 6
U.S. drops atomic bomb on the Japanese city of Hiroshima, killing as many as 140,000 people instantly

AUGUST 8
Soviet Union declares war on Japan

AUGUST 9
U.S. drops an atomic bomb on the Japanese city of Nagasaki, killing more than 80,000 people instantly

AUGUST 14
Japan surrenders

SEPTEMBER 2
Japan signs formal surrender agreement

SEPTEMBER 25
The Nazi Party is declared illegal in Germany

OCTOBER 24
The United Nations is created

NOVEMBER 13
General de Gaulle is elected president of France

NOVEMBER 14
The Nuremberg trials of Nazi leaders for war crimes begin

A more complete time-line, with videos, can be found at the Web site of the National World War II Museum at national-ww2museum.org. Canadian forces' efforts on D-Day are described at the Canadian War Museum Web site warmuseum.ca.

KEY PLAYERS

JOSEPH BALKOSKI: historian, author of *Omaha Beach: D-Day, June 6, 1944*

WILLIAM BLAKE: English poet of the late eighteenth and early nineteenth centuries

OMAR N. BRADLEY: General, field commander in North Africa and Europe, U.S. First Army

DAVID K. E. BRUCE: operative at the U.S. Office of Strategic Services

HARRY C. BUTCHER: commander who served as aide to General Eisenhower from 1942 to 1945

ROBERT CAPA: Hungarian war photographer and photojournalist

WINSTON CHURCHILL: Prime Minister of the United Kingdom of Great Britain and Northern Ireland

J. LAWTON COLLINS: Major General, U.S. Army VII Corps commander

NORMAN D. "DUTCH" COTA: Brigadier General, senior U.S. officer on Omaha Beach

JOSEPH T. DAWSON: Captain, G Company in the U.S. 16th Infantry

MILES DEMPSEY: Lieutenant General, British Second Army commander

MORTON L. DEYO: Rear Admiral, commander of the U.S. Navy gunfire support at Utah Beach

FRIEDRICH DOLLMANN: German General, Seventh Army

FRANK DRAPER, JR.: Sergeant, U.S. Company A, 116th Infantry

DWIGHT D. EISENHOWER: Supreme Commander of the Allied forces in Europe

SIMON FRASER: Lord Lovat, Brigadier, British No. 4 Commando Unit

GORDON GASKILL: invasion correspondent

JAMES M. GAVIN: Brigadier General, assistant commander of the U.S. 82nd Airborne

MARTHA GELLHORN: American journalist and war correspondent; married to Ernest Hemingway from 1940 to 1945

GEORGE VI: King of the United Kingdom and Dominions of the British Commonwealth

ERNEST HEMINGWAY: American writer and war correspondent

ADOLF HITLER: Führer of Germany and leader of the Nazi Party

JOHN HOWARD: Major, British glider force

RANDALL JARRELL: American poet

ALFRED JODL: German General, Chief of the Operations Staff

JOHN KEEGAN: British military historian

EDWARD C. "CANNONBALL" KRAUSE: Lieutenant Colonel, U.S. 3rd Battalion commander

TRAFFORD LEIGH-MALLORY: British Air Chief Marshal, a senior commander in the Royal Air Force

A. J. LIEBLING: war correspondent and writer for the *New Yorker* who witnessed the landing at Omaha Beach

GEORGE MARSHALL: General of the U.S. Army and Chief of Staff

E. J. KINGSTON McCLOUGHRY: Air Vice Marshal, Australian, served in a planning capacity

BILL MILLIN: Piper with the 1st Special Service Brigade

BERNARD L. MONTGOMERY: General, in command of all Allied ground forces during Operation OVERLORD

DON P. MOON: Rear Admiral, U.S. naval commander of Force U

ALAN MOOREHEAD: author and war correspondent for London's *Daily Express*

FREDERICK E. MORGAN: British Lieutenant General, Eisenhower's Chief of Staff, one of the planners of Operation OVERLORD

GEORGE S. PATTON, JR.: General in command of the Third U.S. Army

FORREST C. POGUE: Sergeant, U.S. Army historian

DON F. PRATT: Brigadier General, U.S. 101st assistant division commander

WILLIAM PRESTON: U.S. Corporal

ERNIE PYLE: Pulitzer Prize–winning journalist and war correspondent

BERTRAM RAMSAY: British Admiral, expert in amphibious warfare

MATTHEW B. RIDGWAY: U.S. Major General, division commander of the 82nd Airborne

ERWIN ROMMEL: Field Marshal, commander of German ground forces in the invasion of Normandy

LUCIE–MARIA ROMMEL: Erwin's wife, whose fiftieth birthday drew Rommel away from his post at the time of the invasion

FRANKLIN D. ROOSEVELT: President of the United States from 1933 to 1945

THEODORE ROOSEVELT, JR.: U.S. Brigadier General, led the assault on Utah Beach. (He was the son of President Theodore Roosevelt and was married to Eleanor Butler Alexander.)

GERD VON RUNDSTEDT: Field Marshal of the German army

VERNON SCANNELL: British soldier, poet, and author who took part in D-Day

LOUIS SIMPSON: American poet and gliderman with the 101st Airborne

WALTER BEDELL "BEETLE" SMITH: Lieutenant General, SHAEF chief of staff

J. M. STAGG: Group Captain, British Air Force meteorologist

JOSEPH STALIN: Premier of the Soviet Union

BERT STILES: American writer and bomber pilot

GEORGE A. TAYLOR: Colonel in the U.S. 16th Infantry at Omaha Beach

MAXWELL D. TAYLOR: U.S. Army Major General, the first Allied general to land in France on D-Day

HARRY TRUMAN: President of the United States (became the thirty-third president upon Roosevelt's death on April 12, 1945)

JAMES A. VAN FLEET: Colonel, U.S. Eighth Infantry commander, landed on Utah Beach

EVELYN WAUGH: British officer and writer who served in the Royal Marines

DON WHITEHEAD: American journalist for the Associated Press who landed on Omaha Beach

A NOTE TO READERS

MY FATHER WAS A SOLDIER, which made me an "Army brat." He enlisted in the army when he was eighteen years old, in 1943, about halfway through World War II. He became a lieutenant and arrived in Europe just after the war there ended. A few years later, my father came home to America, went to college, got married, and went back into the army, this time to make it a career. Once again he was sent to war-torn Europe. I was born in Germany, but we lived for several years in Austria, which was still occupied by American troops.

I guess it's no wonder that I have always been fascinated by World War II. It was the worst catastrophe in human history—a time of great heroes, of bravery and sacrifice, but also a time of great villains, of cowardice and horrible crimes. Seventy years after it was fought, the war continues to influence our lives today. Whether or not your great-grandfather or great-grandmother served in the military or worked in a war production factory, chances are it was the most exciting, terrifying, and memorable period of their lives.

World War II is also the greatest story of the twentieth century, and my hope is that you will get to know this story because it tells us a lot about who we are as a nation and what events shaped the world you know today.

Washington, D.C.

THE P

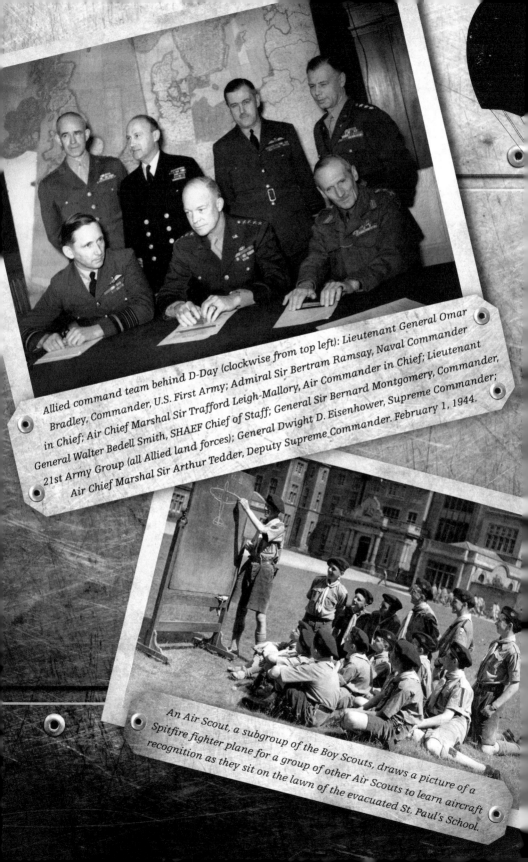

Allied command team behind D-Day (clockwise from top left): Lieutenant General Omar Bradley, Commander, U.S. First Army; Admiral Sir Bertram Ramsay, Naval Commander in Chief; Air Chief Marshal Sir Trafford Leigh-Mallory, Air Commander in Chief; Lieutenant General Walter Bedell Smith, SHAEF Chief of Staff; General Sir Bernard Montgomery, Commander, 21st Army Group (all Allied land forces); General Dwight D. Eisenhower, Supreme Commander; Air Chief Marshal Sir Arthur Tedder, Deputy Supreme Commander. February 1, 1944.

An Air Scout, a subgroup of the Boy Scouts, draws a picture of a Spitfire fighter plane for a group of other Air Scouts to learn aircraft recognition as they sit on the lawn of the evacuated St. Paul's School.

THE
GATHERING
MAY 5, 1944

IN THIS ROOM, the greatest Anglo-American military leaders of World War II gathered to rehearse the deathblow intended to destroy Adolf Hitler's Third Reich. It was the 1,720th day of the war. Admirals, generals, field marshals, logisticians, and staff by the score climbed from their limousines and marched into a Gothic building of St. Paul's School. American military policemen—known as Snowdrops for their white helmets, white pistol belts, white leggings, and white gloves—looked closely at the 146 engraved invitations and security passes distributed a month earlier. Then six uniformed ushers escorted the guests, later described as "big men with the air of fame about them," into the Model Room, a cold auditorium with black columns and hard, narrow benches reputedly designed to keep young schoolboys awake. The students of St. Paul's School had long been evacuated to rural England—German bombs had shattered seven hundred windows across the school's campus.

Top-secret charts and maps now lined the Model Room. Since January, the school had served as headquarters for the British 21st Army Group, and here the detailed planning for Operation OVERLORD, the Allied invasion of France, had gelled. As the senior officers found their benches in rows B through J, some spread blankets across their laps or cinched their overcoats against the chill. Row A, fourteen armchairs arranged elbow to elbow, was reserved for the highest of the mighty, and now these men began to take their seats. The prime minister of England, Winston Churchill, dressed in a black coat and

Air Chief Marshal Sir Sholto Douglass (left) standing with his senior air staff officer in the operations room on the morning of the invasion.

holding his usual Havana cigar, entered with U.S. General Dwight D. Eisenhower, whose title, Supreme Commander of the Allied Expeditionary Force, signaled his leadership over all of the Allied forces in Europe. Neither cheers nor applause greeted them, but the assembly stood as one when King George VI strolled down the aisle to sit on Eisenhower's right. Churchill bowed to his monarch, then resumed puffing his cigar.

*His Imperial Majesty
King George VI*

As they waited to begin at the stroke of ten A.M., these big men with their air of importance had reason to rejoice in their joint victories and to hope for greater victories still to come in this war.

Sir Winston Churchill, prime minister of the United Kingdom, inspecting a crater left by a German bomb in London, September 10, 1940.

Since September 1939, war had raged across Europe, eventually spreading to North Africa and as far east as Moscow, capital of the Soviet Union. Germany, a country humiliated after World War I, had seen the rise of Adolf Hitler, a dictator who had dreams of conquering the continent. Beginning with Poland, his armies had crushed one nation after another, destroying cities and killing or enslaving millions of people. His collaborators in the Axis alliance, particularly Japan and Italy, pushed their own campaigns of aggression in Asia and Africa.

Hitler's invasion of the Soviet Union in June 1941, and Japan's attack in December of that year on the U.S. naval base at Pearl Harbor in Hawaii, led to a grand alliance determined to stop the Axis. The United States, Great Britain, and the Soviet Union were the major Allied powers, but they were supported

Adolf Hitler, führer of the Nazi Party (right), and Benito Mussolini, prime minister of Italy, in Munich, Germany, June 1940.

The U.S.S. Shaw *explodes during the Japanese attack on Pearl Harbor, December 7, 1941.*

by dozens of other countries. At an enormous cost in blood, Soviet armies pushed the German invaders back through eastern Europe, mile by mile. German casualties there exceeded three million, and in 1944 nearly two-thirds of Hitler's combat power remained tied up in the east.

The United States and Britain, meanwhile, had defeated German and Italian forces in North Africa. They then moved north across the Mediterranean Sea to conquer much of Italy, which surrendered and abandoned the Axis. The Third Reich, as Hitler called his empire, was ever more vulnerable to air attack. Allied planes flying from Britain, Italy, and Africa dropped thousands of tons of bombs on Germany and on German forces along various battle fronts. City by city, factory

"TROOPS ARE ONLY GOOD WHEN PUT ASHORE. IT'S OUR JOB TO PUT THEM THERE AND WE WILL."

Vice Admiral R. K. TURNER, U.S.N.
COMMANDER, U. S. NAVAL TASK FORCE, PACIFIC THEATER

DELIVER FOR D DAY!

A U.S. propaganda poster encourages increased production prior to D-Day, 1943–1944.

by factory, Germany was a country increasingly in flames. Although they paid a staggering cost in airplanes and flight crews, the U.S. Army Air Forces, Britain's Royal Air Force, and the Canadian Air Force had won mastery of the European skies, even as Allied navies controlled the seas.

By the late spring of 1944, the Allies were ready to attempt something that had long seemed impossible: to invade what the Germans called "Fortress Europe" and begin the final campaign that would free citizens who had been enslaved since Germany invaded Poland on September 1, 1939. The hour of liberation had nearly arrived.

ON THE EVE OF A GREAT BATTLE:
THE SUPREME ALLIED COMMANDER

General Dwight D. Eisenhower at his headquarters in England.

AT TEN A.M. that Monday, Eisenhower rose to greet the 145 colleagues who would lead the assault on Fortress Europe. Behind him lay an immense plaster relief map of the Normandy coast, a region in France south of England. There the river Seine spilled into the Atlantic. Thirty feet wide and set on a tilted platform visible from the back benches, the map depicted, in bright colors and on a scale of six inches to the mile, the rivers, villages, beaches, and plateaus of what would become the world's most famous battlefield. A brigadier wearing skidproof socks and armed with a pointer stood, ready to indicate locales soon to be known in every household: Cherbourg, St.-Lô, Caen, Omaha Beach.

With only a hint of his famous grin, Eisenhower spoke briefly. He hailed king and comrades alike "on the eve of a great battle," welcoming them to the final check of an invasion blueprint two years in the making. A week earlier he had chosen June 5 as D-Day, the "D" being a coded designation for the day of an important invasion or military operation. "I consider it to be the duty of anyone who sees a flaw in the plan *not* to hesitate to say so," Eisenhower said, his voice booming. "I have no sympathy with anyone, whatever his station, who will not brook criticism. We are here to get the best possible results." The supreme commander would remain preoccupied for some weeks with the sea and air demands of OVERLORD, as well as with other political distractions, so he had delegated the planning and conduct of this titanic land battle in Normandy to the soldier who would now review his battle scheme.

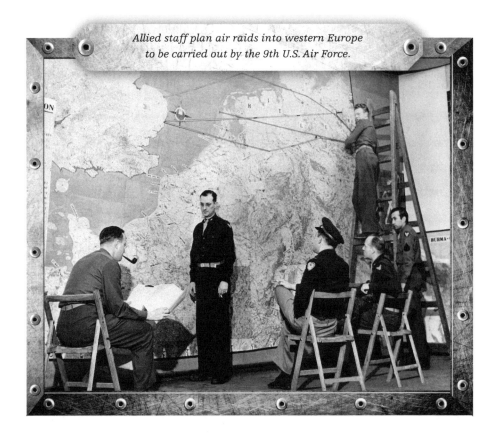

Allied staff plan air raids into western Europe to be carried out by the 9th U.S. Air Force.

PLANNING THE LAND BATTLE:
THE BRITISH HIGH COMMAND

Sir Winston Churchill and Field Marshal Bernard Montgomery, 1944.

A WIRY, elfin figure whose face was among England's most recognizable, attired in immaculate battle dress and padded shoes, popped to his feet, pointer in hand. But before General Bernard L. Montgomery could utter a syllable, a sharp rap sounded. The rap grew bolder; a Snowdrop flung open the Model Room door, and in swaggered George S. Patton, Jr., the hard-driving and outspoken U.S. lieutenant general. Never reluctant to stage an entrance, Patton had swept through London in a huge black Packard car, adorned with three-star insignia and sporting dual Greyhound bus horns. Ignoring Montgomery's scowl, he found his bench in the second row and sat down.

With a curt swish of his pointer, Montgomery stepped to the great floor map. He had been schooled here at St. Paul's. Every morning for four years he had come to this hall to hear prayers in Latin; his office now occupied the High Master's

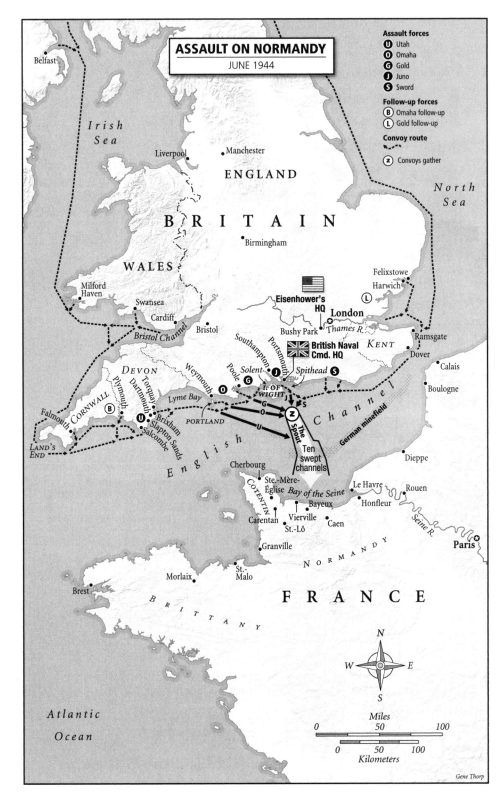

ASSAULT ON NORMANDY
JUNE 1944

Assault forces
U Utah
O Omaha
G Gold
J Juno
S Sword

Follow-up forces
B Omaha follow-up
L Gold follow-up

Convoy route
z Convoys gather

Belfast

Irish Sea

Liverpool Manchester

ENGLAND

North Sea

B R I T A I N

Birmingham

WALES

Felixstowe
Harwich

Milford Haven

Swansea

Cardiff

Bristol

Bristol Channel

Eisenhower's HQ

London
Bushy Park *Thames R.*

British Naval Cmd. HQ

KENT

Ramsgate

Dover

Calais

DEVON

Weymouth

Poole
Solent

Southampton Portsmouth

I. OF WIGHT Spithead S

Boulogne

Plymouth

Torquay

Dartmouth

Lyme Bay

CORNWALL

Brixham
Slapton Sands
Salcombe

PORTLAND

O G J

English Channel

The Spout

German minefield

Dieppe

LAND'S END

Falmouth

B

U

G
O
U

Z

Ten swept channels

Cherbourg

Ste.-Mère-Église

COTENTIN

Bay of the Seine

Le Havre

Honfleur

Rouen

Carentan

Vierville
St.-Lô

Bayeux

Caen

Seine R.

Paris

Granville

NORMANDY

St.-Malo

Morlaix

F R A N C E

Brest

B R I T T A N Y

Atlantic Ocean

N
W E
S

Miles
0   50   100

0   50   100
Kilometers

Gene Thorp

suite, to which he claimed never to have been invited as a boy.

Glancing at his notes—twenty brief items, written in his tidy cursive on unlined stationery—Montgomery began in his reedy voice, each word as sharply creased as his trousers. "There are four armies under my command," he said, two comprising the assault force into Normandy and two more to follow to secure the beachhead.

General George S. Patton, commander of the Third U.S. Army, March 1943.

"We must blast our way on shore and get a good lodgement before the enemy can bring sufficient reserves to turn us out. Armored columns must penetrate deep inland, and quickly, on D-Day. This will upset the enemy plans and tend to hold him off while we build up strength. We must gain space rapidly, and peg out claims well inland."

The Bay of the Seine, which lay within range of almost two hundred fighter airfields in England, had been designated as the invasion site more than a year earlier for both its flat, sandy beaches and its proximity to Cherbourg, a critical port needed to get supplies to the invading forces. True, the Pas de Calais coastline was closer, but it had been deemed "strategically unsound" because the small beaches there were not only exposed to Channel storms but also had become the most heavily defended beaches in France. Planners under the capable British lieutenant general Frederick E. Morgan scrutinized other possible landing sites from Brittany to Holland and found them wanting. Secret missions to inspect the OVERLORD beaches, launched from tiny submarines at night in what the Royal Navy called "impudent reconnaissance," dispelled anxieties about quicksand bogs and other perils. As proof, Commandos brought back Norman sand samples in buckets and test tubes.

Upon returning from Italy five months earlier, Montgomery had widened the OVERLORD assault zone from the twenty-five miles proposed in an earlier plan to fifty miles. Instead of three seaborne divisions, five would lead the assault—two American divisions in the west, two British and one Canadian in the east—preceded seven hours earlier by three airborne divisions to secure the east and west sides of the vast beach and help the forces thrust inland. This grander OVERLORD required 230 additional support ships and landing vessels such as the big LSTs—"landing ship, tank." Assembling that larger

Many LCTs, covered in camouflage netting, await cargo at the port at Southampton, England.

fleet had in turn meant postponing the Normandy invasion from May until early June, and delaying indefinitely an invasion of southern France originally scheduled to occur at the same moment.

As he unfolded his plan, Montgomery walked along the plaster beaches and the tiny Norman villages, head bowed, eyes darting, hands clasped behind his back. Often he repeated himself for emphasis, voice rising the second time. No audience had ever been more rapt, the officers perched on those unforgiving benches, bundled in their blankets and craning their necks. Only Churchill interrupted with mutterings about too many vehicles in the invasion brigades at the expense of too few cutthroat foot soldiers. And was it true, he demanded, that the great force would include two thousand clerks to keep records?

Montgomery pressed ahead. Hitler's so-called Atlantic Wall, the fortified western coast of mainland Europe and Scandinavia, now fell under the command of an old adversary, Field Marshal Erwin Rommel. German divisions in western Europe had nearly doubled since October, from thirty-seven to almost sixty, one reason that Montgomery had insisted on a heftier invasion force. He continued:

Last February, Rommel took command from Holland to the Loire. It is now clear that his intention is to deny any penetration. OVERLORD is to be defeated on the beaches. . . . Rommel is an energetic and determined commander. He has made a world of difference since he took over. He is best at the spoiling attack; his forte is disruption. . . . He will do his level best . . . not to fight the armored battle on ground of his own choosing, but to avoid it altogether by preventing our tanks landing, by using his own tanks well forward.

Some officers in SHAEF—Eisenhower's Supreme Headquarters Allied Expeditionary Force—believed that German resistance might collapse from internal weaknesses, and then OVERLORD would quickly become an occupation force. Montgomery disagreed, and he ticked off the expected enemy counterpunch. Five German divisions, including the 21st Panzer Division, would oppose the invaders on D-Day; by dusk, two other panzer divisions could join the fight, reinforced by two more at the end of D+1, the second day of the invasion, for a total of nine German divisions battling eight Allied divisions ashore. "After a sea voyage and a landing on a strange coast, there is always some loss of cohesion,"

Badge of the Supreme Headquarters Allied Expeditionary Force (SHAEF). Each part of the design is symbolic: The flaming sword pierces the black of Nazi oppression. The rainbow at the top contains all the colors in the flags of the Allied countries.

Montgomery said. A death struggle to amass combat power would determine the battle: OVERLORD's plan called for Allied reinforcements to land at the rate of one and one-third divisions each day, of 7,500 men each. But a bit more than a week into the fight, twenty four German divisions could well try to fling eighteen Allied divisions back into the sea.

Montgomery envisioned a battle beyond the beaches in which the British and Canadian Second Army on the east grappled with the main force of German defenders, while the American First Army on the west surrounded Cherbourg. Three weeks or so after the initial landings, Patton's Third Army would thunder into France, swing through Brittany to capture more ports, and then wheel to the river Seine around D+90, three months into the operation. Paris likely would be liberated in mid-fall, giving the Allies a lodgement between the Seine and the river Loire to prepare for the fateful drive on Germany.

Precisely how that enormous final battle would unfold was difficult to predict even for the clairvoyants at SHAEF. The Combined Chiefs of Staff—Eisenhower's superiors in Washington and London, whom he privately called the Charlie-Charlies—had sent him a thirty-word order: "You will enter the continent of Europe and, in conjunction with the other united nations, undertake operations aimed at the heart of Germany and the destruction of her armed forces." They had instructed him to aim northeast from Normandy toward the Ruhr Valley, the German industrial heartland. SHAEF believed that loss of the Ruhr "would be fatal to Germany"; thus, an assault directed there would set up a decisive battle of annihilation by forcing the enemy to defend the region. Eisenhower also favored an Allied thrust toward the Saar valley, a subsidiary industrial zone farther south; as he had cabled the War Department in early May, a two-pronged attack "would oblige the enemy to extend his forces." To gather power for that ultimate war-winning drive into central Germany, some forty-five Allied divisions and eleven major supply depots would be in position along a front south of Antwerp through Belgium and eastern France by D+270, or roughly early March 1945.

But that lay in the distant future; the immediate task required reaching the far shore. If OVERLORD succeeded, the Normandy assault would dwindle to a mere episode in the larger saga of Europe's liberation. If OVERLORD failed, the entire Allied enterprise faced abject collapse.

It must begin with "an ugly piece of water called the Channel," as the official U.S. Army history would describe it. This waterway between England and France—only twenty-one miles wide at its narrowest—had first been crossed by balloon in 1785, by passenger paddle steamer in 1821, and by a male swimmer in 1875. Yet for nearly a thousand years, invading armies facing a hostile shore across the English Channel had found more grief than glory. The U.S. War Department had even pondered tunneling beneath the seabed: a detailed study deemed the project "feasible," requiring one year and 15,000 men to excavate 55,000 tons of earth and rock. Wiser heads questioned "the strategic and functional" complexities, such as the possibility of the entire German Seventh Army waiting for the first tunneler to emerge. The study was shelved.

Montgomery closed his remarks with his twentieth and final

point, eyes aglint. "We shall have to send the soldiers in to this party seeing red," he declared. "Nothing must stop them. If we send them in to battle this way, then we shall succeed." He knew that men who were "fighting mad" had the best chance of victory.

In quick succession, other senior commanders laid out the naval plan for the invasion, the air plans in both the battle zone and across all German-held lands, the logistics plan, and the civil affairs scheme for governing Normandy. Staff officers scurried about after each presentation, unfurling new maps and swapping out charts.

At 1:30 P.M. the assembly broke for lunch.

At 2:30 the warlords reconvened in the Model Room for

more briefings, more charts, more striding along the painted Norman terrain, this time by the commanders who would oversee the landings, including the senior tactical U.S. Army officer in OVERLORD, Lieutenant General Omar N. Bradley.

Then they were done. Eisenhower stood for a few words of thanks, noting that Hitler had "missed his one and only chance of destroying with a single well-aimed bomb the entire high command of the Allied forces."

Churchill gave a brief valedictory, grasping his coat lapels in both hands. "Let us not expect all to go according to plan. Flexibility of mind will be one of the decisive factors," he said. "Risks must be taken." He bade them all Godspeed.

Never would they be more unified, never more resolved. They came to their feet, shoulders squared, tramping from the hall to the limousines waiting on Hammersmith Road to carry them to command posts across England. Ahead lay the most prodigious undertaking in the history of warfare.

General Eisenhower in the London office.

CONSIDERING THE SOLDIERS

THIRTY MINUTES after leaving St. Paul's, the supreme commander's Cadillac eased past a sentry box and through a gate in the ten-foot stone wall surrounding Bushy Park, an ancient royal preserve tucked into a bend in the Thames River. Majestic chestnut trees swept toward nearby Hampton Court Palace. An entire battalion was in charge of camouflaging this site with nets and green paint, but the shabby, tin-roof huts and a warren of air raid shelters proved difficult to hide. Code-named WIDEWING, the compound served as SHAEF's central headquarters. Here hundreds of staff officers puzzled over challenges they named PINWE issues, for "Problems of the Invasion of Northwest Europe."

Eisenhower's office, designated C-1 and guarded by more Snowdrops, featured a fireplace, a pair of leather easy chairs on a brown carpet, and a walnut desk with framed photos of his mother; his wife, Mamie; and his son, John. His four-star flag stood against one wall, along with a Union Jack, the British flag, and the Stars and Stripes, the flag of the United States. Visitors sometimes found Eisenhower putting an imaginary golf ball across the floor, but now he sat in his swivel chair at the desk. A brimming in-basket and the maroon leather logbook of cables and intelligence reports occupied him into the evening as the furrows deepened on his brow and the mound of cigarette butts grew higher in the ashtray. "How many youngsters are gone forever," Eisenhower had written Mamie in April. "A man must develop a veneer of callousness."

British Empire casualties in the war now exceeded half a million; the sixteen divisions to be committed under Montgomery, including Canadians and Poles, amounted to Churchill's last troop reserves. The usual British casualty

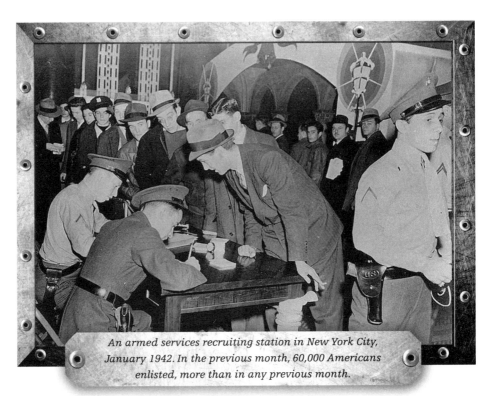

An armed services recruiting station in New York City, January 1942. In the previous month, 60,000 Americans enlisted, more than in any previous month.

forecasts projected three levels of combat: Quiet, Normal, and Intense. But the anticipated carnage in Normandy had led planners to add a new level: Double Intense. According to a British study, enemy fire sweeping a 200-by-400-yard swath of beach for two minutes would inflict casualties above 40 percent on an assault battalion.

American casualties were projected to reach 12 percent of the assault force on D-Day, or higher if gas warfare erupted. The 1st Infantry Division, the point of the spear on Omaha Beach, estimated that under "maximum" conditions, casualties would reach 25 percent, of whom almost a third would be killed, captured, or missing. The rest would sustain injuries that would require their evacuation. The admiral commanding bombardment forces at Utah Beach told his captains that "we might expect to lose one-third to one-half of our ships." Projected U.S. combat drownings in June, exclusive of paratroopers, had been calculated at a grimly precise 16,726.

Recent exercises and rehearsals had not given Eisenhower cause for optimism. Since January, in coves around Britain, troops had been practicing on beaches. A British officer named Evelyn Waugh later wrote, "Sometimes they stood on the beach and biffed imaginary defenders into the hills; sometimes they biffed imaginary invaders from the hills into the sea.... Sometimes they merely collided with imaginary rivals for the use of the main road and biffed them out of the way." Too often, in exercises with names like DUCK, OTTER, and MALLARD, the pretend slugfest proved clumsy and inept. "Exercise BEAVER was a disappointment to all who participated," a secret assessment noted. "The navy and the army and the airborne all got confused." When 529 paratroopers in 28 planes returned to their airfields without jumping during one rehearsal, courts-martial were threatened for "misbehavior in the presence of the enemy," even though the enemy had yet to be met.

The imaginary biffing turned all too real on April 28 in a preparation for D-Day called Exercise TIGER. Through a "series of mistakes and misunderstandings," as investigators later concluded, troop convoy T-4 was left virtually unprotected as it steamed toward Slapton Sands on the south coast of Devon, chosen for its resemblance to Normandy. At two A.M., nine German E-boats (who were not part of the exercise) eluded a British escort twelve miles offshore and torpedoed three U.S. Navy LSTs with such violence that sailors on undamaged vessels

U.S. troops practice disembarking from landing craft and establishing a beachhead on the coast of Devon, England.

A German U-boat

nearby believed *they* had been hit. Fire "spread instantly from stem to stern," a witness reported. Two ships sank, one in seven minutes, disproving talk that torpedoes would pass beneath a shallow-draft LST.

Survivors on rafts sang "Oh, What a Beautiful Mornin'" at first light, but sunrise belied that too. Hundreds of corpses in battle gear drifted on the tide until salvage crews with boat hooks could hoist them from the sea. Forty trucks hauled the dead to a cemetery near London, where all twenty-three licensed British embalmers—their practice was not widespread in the United Kingdom—agreed to help prepare the bodies for burial. Drowned men continued to wash ashore for weeks; the final death toll approached seven hundred. For now the Slapton Sands calamity remained secret.

Eisenhower grieved for the lost men, and no less for the lost LSTs: his reserve of the vital transports now stood at zero. "Not a restful thought," he wrote Marshall.

He needed sleep. Tomorrow would be hectic, beginning with morning meetings at Bushy Park; later he would leave for an inspection trip aboard *Bayonet*, the armored rail coach he used for extended journeys. (Two adjoining boxcars, known as Monsters, carried five sedans, two jeeps, and a small arsenal of guns, while the dining car could seat thirty-two.) By the end of the month he intended to visit more than two dozen divisions, a like number of airfields, and countless warships, depots, and hospitals.

General Dwight D. Eisenhower and Prime Minister Winston Churchill inspect U.S. glider and paratroops in England, March 23, 1944.

AS THE GIs ARRIVE

Military personnel gather in New York City.

BY THE TENS OF THOUSANDS, soldiers in olive drab continued to pour into Britain. Since January the number of GIs had doubled, to 1.5 million, a far cry from the first paltry four thousand in early 1942. Of the U.S. Army's eighty-nine divisions, twenty now could be found in the United Kingdom, with thirty-seven more either en route or earmarked for the European theater. Through Liverpool they arrived, and through Swansea, Cardiff, Belfast, Avonmouth, and Newport. But most came into Glasgow, Scotland, and adjacent Greenock, more than 100,000 in April alone, 15,000 at a time on the two liners—*Queen Elizabeth* and *Queen Mary*—each of which could haul an entire division and outrun German U-boats to make the crossing from New York in five days.

Down the gangplanks they tromped, names checked from a clipboard, each soldier wearing his helmet, his field jacket, and a large button color-coded by the section of the ship to which he had been confined during the passage. Troops carried four blankets apiece to save cargo space, while deluded officers could be seen lugging folding chairs, pillowcases, and tennis rackets. A brass band and Highland pipers greeted them on the dock; Scottish children raised their arms in a *V* for victory. Each arriving unit was listed in a master log called the Iron Book, and another manifest, the Forecast of Destination, showed where every company would bivouac, momentarily, in Britain. As the men fell into columns four abreast and marched from the dock to nearby troop trains, no one needed a forecast to know that they were headed for trouble.

"You are something there are millions of," the poet Randall Jarrell had written without exaggeration. Just over eight million men had been inducted into the U.S. Army and Navy during the past two years—eleven thousand every day. The average GI was twenty-six, born the year that World War I ended, but

U.S. Army nurses wearing full field dress,
ready to disembark in England.

manpower demands in this global struggle meant the force was growing younger: by 1944 nearly half of all American troops arriving to fight in Europe would be teenagers. One in three GIs had only a grade school education, one in four held a high school diploma, and slightly more than one in ten had attended college for at least a semester. War Department Pamphlet 21-13 would assure them that they were "the world's best paid soldiers." A private earned $50 a month, a staff sergeant $96. Any valiant GI awarded the Medal of Honor would receive an extra $2 each month.

The typical soldier stood five feet eight inches tall and weighed 144 pounds, but physical standards had been lowered to accept defects that once would have kept many young men out of uniform. A man with 20/400 vision could now be conscripted if his sight was correctable to at least 20/40 in one eye; to that end, the armed forces would make 2.3 million pairs of eyeglasses for the troops. The old jest that the army no longer examined eyes but instead just counted them had come true. A man could be drafted if he had only one eye, or was completely deaf in one ear, or was missing a thumb or three fingers on either hand, including a trigger finger. Earlier in the war, a draftee had had to possess at least twelve of his original thirty-two adult teeth, but now he could be utterly toothless. After all, the government had drafted a third of all the civilian dentists in the United States; collectively they would extract 15 million teeth, fill 68 million more, and make 2.5 million sets of dentures, enabling each GI to meet the minimum requirement of "masticating the Army ration."

U.S. Eighth Army Air Force crewmen inspect propellers on a twin-engine Lightning aircraft at a U.S. airbase in England.

But what of their souls? What of their ideals and inner beliefs? Few professed to be warriors, or even natural soldiers. Most were "amateurs whose approach to soldiering was aggressively temporary," one officer observed. An April survey in Britain polled enlisted men about what they would ask Eisenhower if given the chance; at least half wanted to know what even the supreme commander could not tell them: when can we go home? Certainly they believed in one another. Camaraderie offered a defense against what novelist-soldier Vernon Scannell called "this drab khaki world" with its "boredom, cold, exhaustion, squalor, lack of privacy, monotony, ugliness and a constant teasing anxiety about the future." Like soldiers

A lieutenant briefs his soldiers about invasion plans at an encampment in England.

throughout time, they would risk all to be considered worthy of their comrades.

And so, four by four by four, they boarded those troop trains on the docks to be hauled to 1,200 camps and 133 airfields across the British Isles.

Nearly 400,000 prefabricated huts and 279,000 tents had been erected to accommodate the American troops, supplementing 112,000 borrowed British buildings and 20 million square feet of storage space.

While waiting to deploy, soldiers had some recreation time. Here, Canadian soldiers watch a baseball game between Canadian and American army teams. The dog, Booby, was the mascot for the Canadian Scottish troops.

INVASION MATÉRIEL

THE LOADING of invasion vessels bound for the far shore had begun on May 4 and intensified as the month wore on. Seven thousand kinds of combat necessities had to reach the Norman beaches in the first four hours, from surgical scissors to bazooka rockets, followed by tens of thousands of tons in the days following. Responsibility for embarkation fell to three military bureaucracies with acronyms evocative of the comedians the Marx Brothers: MOVCO, TURCO, and EMBARCO. Merchant marine captains sequestered in a London basement prepared loading plans with the blueprints of deck and cargo spaces spread on huge tables; wooden blocks scaled to every jeep, cannon, and shipping container were pushed around like chess pieces to ensure a fit. Soldiers in their camps laid out full-sized deck replicas on the ground and practiced wheeling trucks and guns in and out.

In twenty-two British ports, dockworkers called stevedores

Equipment and supplies were gathered all over England. Here, pallets of K rations are loaded onto a barge.

slung pallets and cargo nets into holds and onto decks, loading radios from Pennsylvania, grease from Texas, rifles from Massachusetts. For OVERLORD, the U.S. Army had accumulated 301,000 vehicles, 1,800 train locomotives, 20,000 railcars, 2.6 million small arms, 2,700 artillery pieces, 300,000 telephone poles, and 7 million tons of gasoline, oil, and lubricants. SHAEF had calculated daily combat consumption, from fuel to bullets to chewing gum, at 41.298 pounds per soldier. Sixty million K rations, enough to feed the invaders for a month, were packed in 500-ton bales. Huge U.S. Army railcars known as war flats hauled tanks and bulldozers to the docks, while mountains of ammunition were stacked on car ferries requisitioned from Boston, New York, and Baltimore. The photographer Robert Capa, who would land with the second wave at Omaha Beach, watched as the "giant toys" were hoisted

Vehicles are hoisted aboard a ship at the London docks, May 30, 1944.

aboard. "Everything looked like a new secret weapon," he wrote, "especially from a distance."

Armed guards from ten cartography depots escorted 3,000 tons of maps for D-Day alone, the first of 210 million maps that would be distributed in Europe. Also into the holds went 280,000 charts of bodies of water; street maps for Cherbourg and St.-Lô; many of the one million aerial photos of German defenses, snapped from reconnaissance planes flying at twenty-five feet; and watercolors depicting the view that soldiers would have of their beaches as they approached. Copies of a French atlas pinpointed monuments and cultural treasures, with an attached order from Eisenhower calling for "restraint and discipline" in wreaking havoc. The U.S. First Army battle plan for OVERLORD contained more words than *Gone with the Wind.* For the 1st Infantry Division alone, Field

Order No. 35 had fifteen annexes and eighteen appendices, including a reminder to "drive on right side of road."

Day after night after day, war matériel cascaded onto the wharves: radio receivers by the thousands; carrier pigeons by the hundreds; medals—one hundred Silver Stars and three hundred Purple Hearts—for each major general to award as warranted; and ten thousand "Hagensen packs," canvas bags sewn by sailmakers in lofts across England and stuffed with explosives. A company contracted to deliver ten thousand metal crosses had missed its deadline; instead, Graves Registration units would improvise with wooden markers.

Four hospital ships made ready, "snowy white . . . with many bright new red crosses painted on the hull and painted flat on the boat deck," the reporter Martha Gellhorn noted. Each LST also would carry at least two physicians and twenty navy corpsmen to evacuate casualties, with operating rooms built on the open tank decks—a "cold, dirty trap," in one officer's estimation—and steam tables used to heat twenty-gallon sterilization cans. All told, OVERLORD would gather 8,000 doctors, 600,000 doses of penicillin, fifty tons of sulfa to fight bacteria, and 800,000 pints of blood. Sixteen hundred pallets weighing half a ton each and designed to be

The Purple Heart medal, awarded to U.S. military personnel wounded or killed in action, bears the likeness of George Washington.

dragged across the beaches were packed with enough medical supplies to last medics two weeks.

On Tuesday, May 23, a great migration of assault troops swept toward the English seaside and into a dozen marshaling areas—Americans on the southwest coast, British and Canadians in the south—where the final staging began. Instructions called for each convoy to travel twenty-five miles in two hours, vehicles sixty yards apart, with a ten-minute halt before every even-numbered hour. Military policemen waved traffic through intersections and thatched-roof villages. Soldiers snickered nervously at the new road signs reading ONE WAY. "We sat on a hilltop and saw a dozen roads in the valleys below jammed with thousands of vehicles, men, and equipment moving toward the south," wrote Sergeant Forrest C. Pogue, an army historian.

Two hospital ships at a port in Southern England, 1941.

An American field howitzer unit lines a village street waiting to embark for Normandy.

By late in the week all marshaling camps were sealed, with sentries ordered to shoot absconders. DO NOT LOITER, signs on perimeter fences warned. CIVILIANS MUST NOT TALK TO ARMY PERSONNEL. GIs wearing captured German uniforms and carrying enemy weapons wandered through the bivouacs so troops grew familiar with the look of the enemy. The invasion had begun to resemble "an overrehearsed play," complained the correspondent Alan Moorehead. Fantastic rumors swirled: that British Commandos had taken Cherbourg; that Berlin intended to sue for peace; that a particular unit would be sacrificed in a diversionary attack; that the German armed forces possessed both a death beam capable of incinerating many acres instantly and a vast refrigerating apparatus to create big icebergs in the English Channel. The U.S. military newspaper *Stars and Stripes* tried to calm jumpy soldiers with an article promising that "shock kept the wounded from feeling much pain."

DECOYS AND CAMOUFLAGE

SECURITY REMAINED PARAMOUNT. SHAEF concluded that OVERLORD had little chance of success if the enemy received even forty-eight hours' advance notice, and "any longer warning spells certain defeat." As part of Churchill's demand that security measures be "high, wide, and handsome," the British government in early April imposed a ban that kept the usual 600,000 monthly visitors from approaching coastal stretches along the North Sea, Bristol Channel, and English Channel. Two thousand army counterintelligence agents sniffed about for leaks. Censors fluent in twenty-two languages and armed with X-Acto knives scrutinized soldier letters for indiscretions until, on May 25, all outgoing mail was impounded for ten days as an extra precaution.

Camouflage inspectors roamed through southern England to ensure that the invasion assembly remained invisible to German surveillance planes. Thousands of tons of cinders and

British soldiers stack bombs in a camouflage tent.

sludge oil darkened new roads. Nets—the British alone used one million square yards—concealed tents and huts while even medical stretchers and surgical lockers were slathered with "tone-down paint," either Standard Camouflage Color 1A (dark brown) or SCC 15 (olive drab). Any vehicle stopped for more than ten minutes was to be draped with a net "propped away from the contours of the vehicle."

Deception complemented the camouflage. The greatest prevarication of the war, originally known as "Appendix Y" until given the code name FORTITUDE, tried "to induce the enemy to make faulty strategic dispositions of forces," as the Combined Chiefs requested. Fifteen hundred Allied deceivers used phony radio traffic to suggest that a fictional army with eight divisions in Scotland would attack Norway in league with the Soviets, followed by a larger invasion of France in mid-July through the Pas de Calais, 150 miles northeast of the actual OVERLORD beaches. More than two hundred eight-ton "Big-bobs"—decoy landing craft fashioned from canvas and oil

An inflatable decoy tank used to mislead the Germans about the site of a possible Allied invasion.

drums—had been conspicuously deployed beginning May 20 around the Thames estuary. Transmitters now broadcast the dummy radio hubbub of a phantom 150,000-man U.S. First Army Group, supposedly poised to pounce on the wrong coast in the wrong month.

The British genius for deception furthered the ruse by passing misinformation through more than a dozen German agents, all discovered, all arrested, and all flipped by British intelligence officers. A network of British double agents with code names like GARBO and TRICYCLE embellished the deception, and some five hundred deceitful radio reports were sent from London to enemy spymasters in Madrid and thence to Berlin. The FORTITUDE deception had spawned a German hallucination: enemy analysts now detected seventy-nine Allied divisions staging in Britain, when in fact there were only fifty-two. By late May, Allied intelligence, including Ultra, the project that intercepted and deciphered coded German radio traffic, had uncovered no evidence suggesting "that the enemy has accurately assessed the area in which our main assault is to be made," as Eisenhower learned to his relief.

JUNE ARRIVES

AS MAY SLID TOWARD JUNE, invasion preparations grew feverish. Every vehicle to be shoved onto the French coast required waterproofing to a depth of fifty-four inches with a gooey compound of grease, lime, and asbestos fibers; a vertical funnel from each exhaust pipe "stuck up like a wren's tail" to keep the engine from flooding. A single Sherman tank took three hundred man-hours to waterproof, occupying the five-man crew for a week. On May 29, SHAEF also ordered all eleven thousand Allied planes to display three broad white stripes on each wing as recognition symbols. A frantic search for a hundred thousand gallons of whitewash and twenty thousand brushes required mobilizing the British paint industry, and workers toiled through weekends. Some aircrews slathered on the white stripes with push brooms.

Soldiers packed seasickness pills, vomit bags, and life belts, incidentals that brought the average rifleman's combat

U.S. troops and vehicles pour into the open mouths of landing ships at Brixham, England, in June 1944.

load to 68.4 pounds, far beyond the 43 pounds recommended for assault troops. A company commander with the 116th Infantry, bound for Omaha Beach, reported that his men were "loping and braying about the camp under their packs, saying that as long as they were loaded like jackasses they may as well sound like them." On June 2, the men donned "skunk suits," stiff, foul-smelling uniforms heavily impregnated against poison gas.

"We're ready now—as ready as we'll ever be," Brigadier General Theodore Roosevelt, Jr., of the 4th Infantry Division, wrote on May 30 to his wife, Eleanor.

Eisenhower left Bushy Park on Friday, June 2, for his war camp, code-named SHARPENER. Trailers and tents filled Sawyer's Wood five miles northwest of Portsmouth Harbor. Eisenhower's personal "circus wagon" featured a bunk and a desk, with the usual stack of western novels and three telephones, including a red one to Washington and a green one to Churchill's underground Map Room in Whitehall. A mile distant down a cinder path stood a three-story Georgian mansion. Originally requisitioned by the Royal Navy for a navigation school—nautical almanacs still stood in the bookcases—Southwick House now served as British Admiral Bertram Ramsay's headquarters and a convenient secure location from which Eisenhower could watch OVERLORD unspool.

General Eisenhower, General de Gaulle (the taller of the two men with backs to the photographer), and Winston Churchill at Southwick House on June 3 or 4, 1944.

Aerial photograph showing ships massing off the Isle of Wight before heading for the Normandy beaches.

A leafy hilltop near Southwick House offered a stunning panorama of the thousand-ship fleet now ready for launching from Spithead and the Solent, a sheltered strait separating the Isle of Wight from the English mainland. Thousands more— the OVERLORD armada numbered nearly seven thousand, including landing craft and barges—filled every berth in every port from Felixstowe on the North Sea to Milford Haven in Wales, with others moored in the Humber, the Clyde, and Belfast Lough.

Soldiers still braying and bleating under their combat loads tramped up gangplanks or through the yawning bow doors of LSTs grounded on concrete pads at the water's edge.

"Have a good go at it, mates," the leathery stevedores called. Others crammed into lighters, flat-bottomed barges, for a short, wet ride out to troopships anchored offshore. British soldiers, called Tommies, heated cocoa and oxtail soup on the decks; a platoon commander marveled at being served "real white bread, which we hadn't seen in years." In Plymouth, where the *Mayflower* left for the New World, so many vessels stood lashed gunwale to gunwale that "a man could have jumped from one deck to another and walked a half-mile up the Tamar River," an American lieutenant reported.

More than five hundred weather stations were scattered across the United Kingdom, most reporting hourly. Eight U.S.

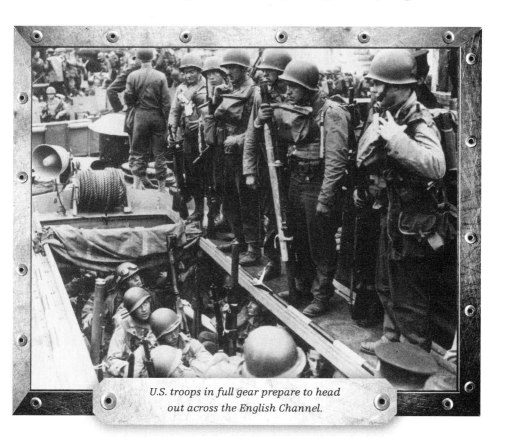

U.S. troops in full gear prepare to head out across the English Channel.

Navy ships also took meteorological readings in the western Atlantic, and reconnaissance planes packed with instruments flew every day from Scotland, Cornwall, and Gibraltar. British beach watchers at fifty-eight wave observation stations noted the height of every breaker during specific three-minute intervals, then sent their reports to a Swell Forecast Section three times a day. Six esteemed forecasters in England conferred twice each day by phone to discuss, often heatedly, the mysteries of wind, cloud, surf, and swell.

Each Allied invasion constituent had particular weather demands. Amphibious forces needed offshore surface winds not greater than Force 4—thirteen to eighteen miles per hour—for three consecutive days, as well as good tides. Pilots wanted a cloud ceiling of at least 2,500 feet for transport planes, with visibility of no less than three miles, and, for heavy bombers, no overcast thicker than the partly cloudy condition designated 5/10. Paratroopers required surface winds below twenty miles an hour, without gusts, and illumination of not less than a half moon at a thirty-degree altitude. The odds against such conditions aligning on the Norman coast for seventy-two hours in June were calculated at thirteen to one.

At 4:30 A.M. on Sunday, June 4, in the high-ceilinged Southwick House library, a somber Eisenhower sat with Montgomery, Ramsay, British Air Chief Marshal Trafford Leigh-Mallory, and half a dozen other senior officers on two couches and a cluster of easy chairs. Beyond a set of French doors blanketed in blackout drapes, an immense map of southern England and Normandy covered one wall, with convoys and divisions depicted by pushpins that two uniformed clerks periodically

Air Chief Marshal Sir Trafford Leigh-Mallory addresses
crews of the Glider Pilot Regiment at an England
airfield after an invasion exercise, May 11, 1944.

adjusted from a stepladder. Standing ill at ease before the supreme commander was a tall officer with a long face. Group Captain J. M. Stagg, a specialist in terrestrial magnetism and solar radiation, regretted to say that, as SHAEF's chief meteorologist, he was altering his grim forecast for the worse.

"A series of depressions across the Atlantic is moving rapidly eastward," Stagg reported. "These depressions will produce disturbed conditions in the Channel and assault area." Weather charts resembled conditions typical of midwinter rather than early summer; depression L5, now skulking toward the Shetland Islands, would produce the lowest atmospheric pressure recorded in the British Isles during June in the twentieth century. In a few hours, complete overcast would blanket southern England, with a ceiling as low as five hundred feet and westerly winds up to thirty miles an hour at Force 6. Conditions for D-Day on June 5 had deteriorated from "most unpromising" to "quite impossible."

Eisenhower polled his lieutenants. "No part of the air support plan would be practicable," Leigh-Mallory told him. Even Ramsay concurred; at Force 6, waves could be six feet or higher. Eisenhower nodded. "We need every help our air superiority can give us," he said. "If the air cannot operate, we must postpone." Only Montgomery disagreed. Conditions would be severe, but *not* impossible. He, for one, was willing to gamble.

At that moment the lights failed. Aides hurried in with candles that outlined the exasperation in Eisenhower's face. According to a subsequent account by Air Vice Marshal E. J. Kingston McCloughry, he snapped at Montgomery, "Here you have been telling us for the past three or four months that you must have adequate air cover and that the airborne operations are essential to the assault, and now you say you will do without them. No, we will postpone OVERLORD twenty-four hours." The conference dissolved. Eisenhower stalked back to his trailer to read the Sunday papers between fitful naps.

As anchors dropped and engines died, taut nerves led to bickering and a few fistfights. Officers tried to keep their men occupied by distributing *A Pocket Guide to France*, a War Department tract that explained the worthiness of the nation to be liberated. Soldiers also learned that "Normandy looks rather like Ohio," that a hectoliter equaled twenty-two gallons, and that the French were "good talkers and magnificent cooks." Troops studying an army phrase book murmured the hopeful

A soldier from the U.K. 101st Light Anti-Aircraft Regiment prepares for D-Day by reading his French handbook, May 29, 1944.

"Encore un verre de vin rouge, s'il vous plaît, mademoiselle," "Another glass of red wine, please, miss." Many GIs attended Sunday church services belowdecks. In the main mess aboard U.S.S. *Bayfield*, soldiers and sailors bellowed out "Holy God, We Praise Thy Name," while a chaplain in Weymouth took his text from Romans 8: "If God be for us, who can be against us?"—an unsettling theological presumption at the moment. Dice and cards reappeared. A combat surgeon described playing "blackjack for twenty dollars a card with officers from headquarters company. I either go into this fight loaded or broke. What's the difference?"

At 9:30 P.M., the supreme commander returned with his lieutenants to the library, where a fire crackled in the hearth and momentous news from Stagg brightened the day's gloom. "There have been some rapid and unexpected developments," the meteorologist reported. H.M.S. *Hoste*, a weather frigate cruising seven hundred miles west of Ireland, reported in secret dispatches that atmospheric surface pressure was rising steadily. The offending Atlantic depressions, including the dismal L5, had moved quicker than expected, suggesting that a brief spell of better weather would arrive the following day and last into Tuesday. "I am quite confident that a fair interval will follow tonight's front," Stagg added.

Eisenhower polled his subordinates once more. Further postponement would likely delay the invasion for nearly two weeks, when the tides next aligned properly. Leigh-Mallory remained skeptical. Bombing would be "chancy," and spotting for naval gunfire difficult. Ramsay reported "no misgivings at all." The SHAEF chief of staff, Lieutenant General Walter Bedell "Beetle" Smith, said, "It's a helluva gamble, but it's the best possible gamble." Eisenhower turned to Montgomery.

"Do you see any reason for not going Tuesday?"

Montgomery answered instantly. "I would say go."

For a long minute the room fell silent but for rain lashing the french doors. Eisenhower stared vacantly, rubbing his head. "The question is, how long can you hang this operation on the end of a limb and let it hang there?" The tension seemed to drain from his face. "I'm quite positive we must give the order," he said. "I don't like it, but there it is. I don't see how we can possibly do anything else." They would reconvene before dawn on Monday, June 5, to hear Stagg's latest forecast, but the order would stand. "Okay," Eisenhower declared. "We'll go."

U.S. Navy sailors review plans for the invasion of Normandy, June 1944.

An American paratrooper in full gear boards his aircraft.

U.S. assault troops load onto a ship.

Troop and supply ships amass near the Isle
of Wight to cross the English Channel.

UP
ANCHOR
JUNE 5, 1944

ACROSS THE FLEET the war cry sounded: "Up anchor!" In the murky dawn, from every English harbor and estuary the ships came converging on the white-capped Channel: nearly 200,000 seamen and merchant mariners crewing 59 convoys carrying 130,000 soldiers, 2,000 tanks, and 12,000 vehicles. "Ships were heaving in the gray waves," wrote war correspondent Alan Moorehead. Monday's early light revealed cutters, corvettes, frigates, freighters, ferries, trawlers, tankers, submarine chasers; ships for channel-marking, for cable-laying, for smoke-making; ships for refrigerating and towing. From the Irish Sea the bombardment squadrons rounded Land's End in pugnacious columns of cruisers, battleships, destroyers, and even some

dreadnoughts given a second life, like the U.S.S. *Nevada*, raised and remade after Pearl Harbor, and the ancient monitor H.M.S. *Erebus*, built to shell German fortifications in World War I with two 15-inch guns of dubious reliability.

By midmorning the heavy skies lightened and the wind quieted and the sea turned from gray to sapphire. A luminous rainbow, said to be "tropical in its colors," arced above the wet, green English fields, and dappled sun lit the chalk cliffs of Kent, turning them into white curtains.

Leading the fleet was the largest minesweeping operation in naval history. Some 255 vessels began by clearing Area Z, a circular swath of sea below the Isle of Wight that was ten miles in diameter. From here the minesweepers sailed through eight corridors that angled to a German minefield in mid-Channel, where a week earlier Royal Navy launches had secretly planted underwater sonic beacons in thirty fathoms. Electronically dormant until Sunday, the beacons now summoned the sweepers to the entrances of ten channels, each of which was four hundred to twelve hundred yards wide; these channels would be cleared for thirty-five miles to five beaches in Normandy. Seven-foot waves and a cross-tidal current of nearly three knots bedeviled helmsmen who fought their wheels, the wind, and the sea to keep on track. As the sweepers swept, more boats followed to lay a lighted buoy every mile on either side of each channel, red to starboard, white to port. The effect, one reporter observed, was "like street lamps across to France."

As the invasion convoys swung toward Area Z, the churlish

open Channel tested the seaworthiness of every landing vessel. Flat-bottomed LSTs showed "a capacity for rolling all ways at once," and the smaller LCI—landing craft, infantry—revealed why it was widely derided as a Lousy Civilian Idea. Worse yet was the LCT—landing craft, tank—capable of only six knots in quiet water and half that in a rough sea. Even the navy acknowledged that "the LCT is not an ocean-going craft due to poor sea-keeping facilities, low speed, and structural weakness"; the latter quality included being bolted together in three sections so that the vessel "gave an ominous impression of being liable to buckle in the middle." Miserable passengers

On the way to the French coast, LSTs tow gas-filled barrage balloons as obstacles against low-flying German planes.

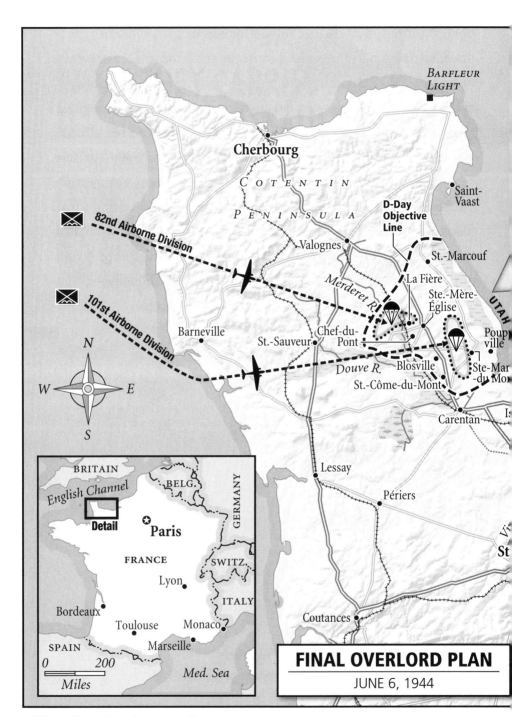

FINAL OVERLORD PLAN

JUNE 6, 1944

Additional map legend on page vii

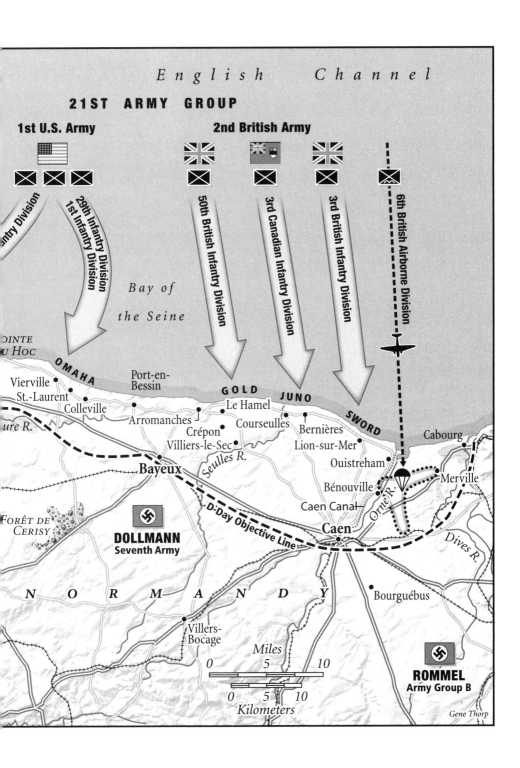

English Channel

21ST ARMY GROUP

1st U.S. Army

2nd British Army

29th Infantry Division
1st Infantry Division

...ntry Division

50th British Infantry Division

3rd Canadian Infantry Division

3rd British Infantry Division

6th British Airborne Division

Bay of
the Seine

POINTE
DU HOC

OMAHA

Vierville
St.-Laurent
Colleville

Port-en-
Bessin

GOLD

JUNO

SWORD

...ure R.

Arromanches

Le Hamel
Courseulles
Bernières
Lion-sur-Mer

Cabourg

Crépon
Villiers-le-Sec

Bayeux

Seulles R.

Ouistreham

Bénouville

Caen Canal

Merville

Orne R.

FORÊT DE
CERISY

DOLLMANN
Seventh Army

D-Day Objective Line

Caen

Dives R.

N O R M A N D Y

Bourguébus

Villers-
Bocage

Miles

0   5   10

ROMMEL
Army Group B

0   5   10
Kilometers

Gene Thorp

traded seasickness remedies, such as one sailor's advice to "swallow a pork chop with a string, then pull it up again."

For those who could eat, pork chops were in fact served to the 16th Infantry, with ice cream. Aboard the *Thomas Jefferson*, 116th Infantry troops headed for Omaha Beach ate what one officer described as "bacon and eggs on the edge of eternity." Soldiers primed grenades, sharpened blades, and field-stripped their rifles, again; a navy physician recommended a good washing to sponge away skin bacteria, "in case you stop one." Some Yanks sang "Happy D-Day, dear Adolf, happy D-Day to you," but Tommies preferred "Jerusalem," based on William Blake's bitter poem set to music: "Bring me my bow of burning gold." Sailors broke out their battle ensigns, the flags that are hoisted just before battle, and converted mess tables into hospital operating theaters. In watertight

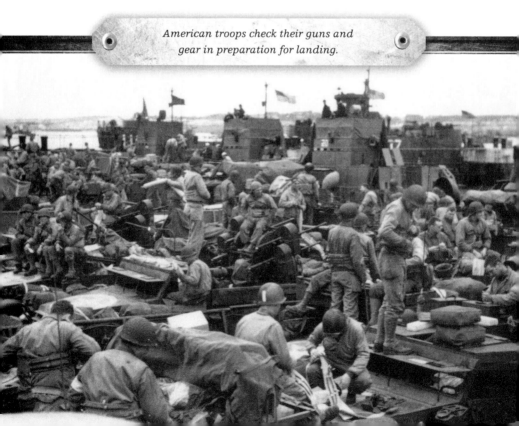

American troops check their guns and gear in preparation for landing.

compartments belowdecks, crewmen aboard the resurrected *Nevada* stowed "dress blues, china, glassware, library books, tablecloths, office files, brooms, mirrors." A Coast Guard lieutenant noted in his diary, "Orders screeched over the PA system for Mr. Whozits to report to Mr. Whatzits in Mr. Wherezits' stateroom." Rear Admiral Morton L. Deyo, aboard U.S.S. *Tuscaloosa* as commander of the Utah Beach bombardment squadron, hammered a punching bag in his cabin.

To inspire the men, officers read stand-tall messages from Eisenhower and Montgomery, then offered their own advice. "The first six hours will be the toughest," Colonel George A. Taylor of the 16th Infantry told reporters on the *Samuel Chase*. "They'll just keep throwing stuff onto the beaches until something breaks. That is the plan."

Brigadier General Norman D. "Dutch" Cota, who would be the senior officer on Omaha Beach on Tuesday morning, told officers aboard the U.S.S. *Charles Carroll*: "You're going to find confusion. The landing craft aren't going in on schedule and people are going to be landed in the wrong place. Some won't be landed at all. . . . We must improvise, carry on, not lose our heads. Nor must we add to the confusion."

A tank battalion commander was more succinct: "The government paid $5 billion for this hour. Get to hell in there and start fighting." Standing on the forecastle of *Augusta*, Omar Bradley flashed a *V* for victory to each wallowing LST before retiring to an armchair in his cabin.

"We are starting on the great venture of this war," Ted Roosevelt wrote Eleanor from the U.S.S. *Barnett*. "The men are crowded below or lounging on deck. Very few have seen action."

Roosevelt, who at fifty-six would be the senior officer on Utah Beach for the first hours in both age and rank, had seen enough—in France during the last war, and in the landings at Oran in Algeria and Gela in Sicily during this one—to have premonitions:

> *We've had a grand life and I hope there'll be more. Should it chance that there's not, at least we can say that in our years together we've packed enough for ten ordinary lives. We've known joy and sorrow, triumph and disaster, all that goes to fill the pattern of human existence. . . . Our feet were placed in a large room, and we did not bury our talent in a napkin.*

Back on deck he told men from the 8th Infantry, "I'll see you tomorrow morning, 6:30, on the beach."

Far inland, at more than a dozen airfields scattered across England, some twenty thousand parachutists and glider troops also made ready. Soldiers from the British 6th Airborne Division blackened their faces with soot while awaiting the order to enplane. "I gave the earth by the runway a good stamp," one private reported.

American paratroopers smeared their skin with cocoa and linseed oil or with charcoal raked from campfires along the taxiways. Every man was overburdened, from the burlap strips woven in the helmet net to the knife with a brass-knuckle grip tucked into the jump boots. Also: parachute, reserve chute, inflatable life jacket, entrenching tool, rations, fragmentation and smoke grenades, blasting caps, TNT blocks,

General Eisenhower gives his last-minute orders, "Full victory—nothing else," to U.S. paratroopers in the 502nd Parachute Infantry Regiment just before they load into planes in England to be dropped behind enemy lines in France, June 5, 1944.

brass pocket compass, signal clicker called a cricket, raincoat, blanket, bandoliers to hold ammunition, rifle, cigarette carton, and morphine syrettes (directions: "one for pain and two for eternity"). Carrier pigeons were stuffed into extra GI socks—their heads poking out of little holes cut in the toe—and fastened to combat jackets with blanket pins. Some officers trimmed the margins from their maps in order to carry a few more rounds of ammunition.

"We look all pockets, pockets and baggy pants. The only visible human parts are two hands," wrote Louis Simpson, the poet-gliderman. "The letter writers are at it again," he continued, "heads bowed over their pens and sheets of paper." Among the scribblers and the map trimmers was the thirty-seven-year-old assistant commander of the 82nd Airborne, Brigadier

Glidermen of the British 1st Airborne giving the V for victory sign. This photo was taken after the initial invasion.

General James M. Gavin, who confessed in a note to his young daughter, "I have tried to get some sleep this afternoon but to no avail." The impending jump likely would be "about the toughest thing we have tackled," added Gavin, whose exploits on Sicily were among the most famous from the Mediterranean theater. In his diary, he was more explicit: "Either this 82nd Division job will be the most glorious and spectacular episode in our history or it will be another Little Big Horn. There is no way to tell now. . . . It will be a very mean and nasty fight."

The prospect of "another Little Big Horn," a battle in which the U.S. Army was vastly outnumbered, particularly for the two American airborne divisions ordered to France despite Leigh-Mallory's dire warning, gnawed at Eisenhower in these final hours. After watching British troops board their LCIs from South Parade Pier in Portsmouth, he had returned to SHARPENER to pass the time playing fox-and-hounds on a checkerboard with his aide commander, Harry Butcher, then sat down to compose a contrite note of responsibility, just in case. "Our landings in the Cherbourg-Havre area have failed to gain a satisfactory foothold and I have withdrawn the troops," he wrote. "If any blame or fault attaches to the attempt it is mine alone." Misdating the paper "July 5"— symptomatic of exhaustion and anxiety—he slipped it into his wallet, for use as needed.

Just after six P.M., Eisenhower climbed into his Cadillac leading a three-car convoy, and rolled north for ninety minutes on narrow roads clogged with military trucks. At Greenham Common airfield in the Berkshire Downs, outside the eleventh-century town of Newbury, he bolted down a quick supper in the headquarters mess of the 101st Airborne, then drove to the flight line. Hands in his pockets, he strolled among the C-47s, newly striped with white paint. Troopers with blackened faces and heads shaved or clipped Mohawk-style wiggled into their parachute harnesses and sipped a final cup of coffee. "The trick is to keep moving. If you stop, if you start thinking, you lose your focus," Eisenhower told a young soldier from Kansas. "The idea, the perfect idea, is to keep moving."

At aircraft number 2716, he shook hands with the division

commander, Major General Maxwell D. Taylor, who was careful to conceal a bad limp from the tendon he had injured playing squash the previous day. Eisenhower wished him Godspeed, then returned to the headquarters manor house and climbed to the roof for a final glimpse of his men. "The light of battle," he would write Army Chief of Staff George Marshall, "was in their eyes." To his driver he confessed, "I hope to God I know what I'm doing."

Red and green navigation lights twinkled across the downs as the sun set at 10:06 P.M. Singing voices drifted in the twilight—"Give me some men who are stout-hearted men / Who will fight for the right they adore"—punctuated by a guttural roar from paratroopers holding their knives aloft in homicidal resolve. Into the airplane bays they heaved themselves, with a helpful shove from behind. Many knelt on the floor to rest their cumbersome gear and chutes on a seat, faces bathed by the soft glow of cigarette embers and red cabin lights. "Give me guts," one trooper prayed. "Give me guts." Engines coughed and caught, the feathered propellers popping as crew chiefs slammed the doors.

From the west the last gleam of a dying day glinted off the aluminum fuselages. "Stay, light," a young soldier murmured, "stay on forever, and we'll never get to Normandy."

The light faded and was gone. Deep into the Channel, fifty-nine darkened convoys went to battle stations as they pushed past the parallel rows of dim buoys, red to starboard, white to port. "Our flag bridge is dead quiet," Admiral Deyo wrote on *Tuscaloosa*. An officer on *Quincy* noted, "This is like trying to slip into a room where everyone is asleep."

Small craft struggled in the wind. "Men sick, waves washed over deck," an LCT log recorded. "Stove went out, nothing to eat, explosives wet and could not be dried out." The seas snapped tow ropes, flooded engine rooms, and sloshed through troop compartments. Several heaving vessels blinkered a one-word message: "Seasick. Seasick. Seasick."

Down the ten channels they plunged, two designated for each of the five forces steaming toward five beaches code-named Utah, Omaha, Gold, Juno, and Sword. Wakes braided and rebraided. The amber orb of a full moon rose through a thinning overcast off the port bow.

Troops and crewmen on board a coast guard landing craft as it approaches Normandy.

BY AIR—
JUMPERS
AND GLIDERS
JUNE 6, 1944

STARS GLINTED on a long column of eight hundred airplanes ferrying thirteen thousand American paratroopers to battle. South they flew—and low, skimming the inky Channel. Dead ahead in the moonlight lay the Cotentin Peninsula, famed for cattle and swarming with Germans. Jumpmasters barked above the engine drone, ordering the men to their feet. With a *click* the sixteen or seventeen jumpers in each bay snapped their parachutes to static lines running overhead. Shortly after one A.M., a captain standing in the slipstream of an open doorway peered down at the white surf beating against a beach. "Say hello to France!" he shouted. Red lights flashed to warn that four minutes ahead lay the drop zones—three tight ovals for the 101st Airborne Division in the lead, three more for the 82nd Airborne close behind.

Then France vanished. A gray cloud bank, unexpected and so thick that pilots could barely see their own wingtips,

Gliders get ready for a foray into western Europe, September 1944.

swallowed planes, then groups of planes. Formations disintegrated as the C-47 Dakotas climbed and dove to avoid colliding. Dark patches of earth swam up through the murk only to disappear, and now German antiaircraft fire—like "so many lighted tennis balls," in one witness's description—began to rip into the clouds. Searchlight beams and magnesium flares drenched the cockpits in molten light, dazzling pilots who lurched left and right despite orders forbidding evasive turns. Enemy tracers created smoke or light that showed the path of antiaircraft fire. Shells blew through aluminum skins as if "someone threw a keg of nails against the side of the airplane." Three GIs died when a smoking two-foot hole opened in a fuselage; a dozen others became so entangled after slipping on the vomit-slick floor that they would return to England without jumping.

Even as the cloud bank thinned to the east, bewildered crewmen mistook one French village for another. Some of the pathfinders who had parachuted an hour earlier either missed the drop zones they were supposed to illuminate—using electronic transmitters and seven signal lamps arranged in a beckoning *T*—or else found enemy troops infesting the ground. Green jump lights began to flash in the aircraft bays anyway. Some flashed too soon, others too late, dumping howling paratroopers into the sea. Cargo bundles got stuck in aircraft doors, delaying the line of troopers for two miles or more. Other planes failed to descend to the specified jump height of 500 feet, or to slow to 110 miles an hour; chutes ripped open with such violence that "anything in my jump pants pockets simply burst through the reinforced bottom seams," a trooper recalled. Rations, grenades, extra underwear, and cooing pigeons spilled out. Gunfire thickened "like a wall of flame." Rather than half a minute, "the trip down took a thousand years," a private later told his family. One chute snagged on a vertical stabilizer, the fin at the back of the plane, and dragged the flailing jumper into the night; another soldier hurtled earthward beneath burning shreds of silk. Men in parachutes that failed to open hit the ground with a sound likened by one soldier to "watermelons falling off the back of a truck."

"I pulled up my knees to make myself as small a target as

British Horsa gliders and parachutes near Caen.

possible," a trooper in the 507th Parachute Infantry wrote. "I pulled on my risers [parachute straps] to try to slip away from the fire." Flames licked through the cabin of a C-47 as frantic soldiers dove out the door before the plane crashed. Most of the jumpers survived; the crew did not.

A burning building near St.-Côme-du-Mont gave German defenders enough illumination to fatally shoot a battalion commander, his executive officer, and a company commander before they touched France. Three other company commanders were captured.

OPERATION
ALBANY

OPERATION ALBANY, the U.S. 101st Airborne mission, was intended to seize four elevated roadways, each roughly a mile apart, leading from Utah Beach to the Cotentin Peninsula interior. American planners knew that marshlands behind the sea dunes had been flooded with two to four feet of water by German engineers, who dammed eight small streams with boulders and tree branches to isolate any invaders arriving on the coastline. Planners did *not* know that the flooding was in fact far more ambitious. Canals, dams, and locks in the southeast Cotentin Peninsula drained the watershed of the Douve and Merderet Rivers, creating pasture for the area's famous cows. Beginning in late 1942, German occupiers closed some floodgates and opened others, allowing tidal surges to create an inland sea ten miles long and up to ten feet deep. Reeds and marsh grass now grew so dense that not even the one million aerial photographs snapped by Allied reconnaissance planes had revealed that there was substantial water under the vegetation. No one was more surprised than the many flailing paratroopers who, upon arriving over the coast of France, had removed their life vests in the airplane bays—only to be pulled to watery graves by their heavy gear.

At four A.M., as thousands of lost and scattered parachutists blundered about in the dark, the first fifty-two gliders carrying troops and heavy equipment arrived "like a swarm of ravens," according to one German description. Most were fifty-foot Wacos, each so flimsy "you could shoot an arrow through it," as a captain admitted, especially without the hardened nose caps ordered in February but yet to arrive. Cut

A daytime drop later in the war.

loose from their tow planes, they drifted to earth; pilots who had rarely—if ever—flown at night felt for the unseen ground while bullets punctured the gliders' fabric skins. Some found the landing zone near Blosville, while others found stone walls, tree trunks, dozing livestock, or antiglider stakes. All eight men in a 101st Airborne surgical team were injured in a crash. A Waco with a large "1" painted on the nose skipped downhill on wet grass for eight hundred feet before smashing into a sycamore tree, breaking both legs of the pilot and killing the copilot; in its cargo bay, as if napping in his jeep, sat the 101st assistant division commander, Brigadier General Don F. Pratt, dead from a broken neck. Survivors kicked through the glider fabric—"like bees out of a hive they came from that hole," a witness reported—and began to salvage the small bulldozer, antitank guns, and medical supplies now on Norman soil.

Of more than six thousand jumpers from the 101st Airborne, barely one thousand had landed on or near the H-hour objectives on this Tuesday morning. Most of the fifteen-hundred-odd jumpers who had drifted far beyond the eight-mile square enclosing the division drop zones would be killed or captured; a few made their way to safety with maps torn from local telephone books by French farmers. More than half of all supply bundles dropped from aircraft lay beyond retrieval at the bottom of various water meadows, with a devastating loss of radios, mortars, and eleven of twelve short cannons called howitzers.

Yet stalwart men, those stout-hearts celebrated in song, gathered themselves to press on. An officer pounding on a farmhouse door to ask directions announced in his best French, *"L'invasion est arrivée"*; a voice from the second-floor window replied, *"Très bien."* The 101st's commander, Major General Taylor, wandered in the dark on his gimpy leg with a drawn pistol, clicking his cricket, collecting lost paratroopers,

and politely declining the ancient rifle offered by a French farmer who said, *"Allez me tuer un Boche."* "Go kill me a German." In the first apricot glow of dawn, Taylor recognized the silhouette of Ste.-Marie-du-Mont's eleventh-century church with gargoyle drainpipes protruding from the stone tower. While paratroopers and Germans exchanged gunfire in the belfry and around the confessional, Taylor sent a small force east to Pouppeville to rout the enemy garrison house by house and seize the southernmost causeway exit from Utah Beach. Three miles north, the 3rd Battalion of the 502nd Parachute Infantry did the same with the two northern causeways.

Five hours after leaping into Normandy, paratroopers lined the sandy ridge overlooking the flooded marshes behind the dunes, waiting for twelve convoys carrying the 32,000 troops in Force U to emerge from the sea.

No objective was more important than Ste.-Mère-Église for the 82nd Airborne as the division's six thousand men swooped over Normandy an hour behind the 101st. Roads from all compass points converged here, and the trunk cable linking Cherbourg in the north with Carentan in the south passed through Ste.-Mère. Unless it held the town, the 82nd had "almost no chance to sustain offensive operations across the Merderet River and to the westward," a regimental study had concluded. Thus, the division drop zones were clustered around this drowsy medieval crossroads of a thousand souls.

OPERATION
BOSTON

ALAS, THE DROPS in the U.S. 82nd Airborne operation BOS-
TON proved even more scattered than those of ALBANY. Paratroopers sifted to earth as far as fifteen miles north of their
intended zones and twenty-five miles south; those too far
afield east and west plunged into the Atlantic and vanished.
Fewer than half of the following gliders landed within a mile of
the air drop target zone, and many were demolished, with dire
losses of antitank guns and other heavy gear. Brigadier General James M. Gavin floated into an apple orchard and spent
the early hours of June 6 with his M-1 rifle in hand, shoving
whatever men he could round up toward the critical Merderet
bridges at La Fière and Chef-du-Pont. Soldiers stripped naked
in the moonlight to dive for equipment bundles in the muddy
fens. A German train captured in the Chef-du-Pont station
yielded only Norman cheese and empty bottles. One gunfight
along the Merderet grew so frenzied that paratroopers not

only shot down enemy soldiers but also slaughtered livestock in a barn. A lieutenant leading a patrol bayoneted three wounded Germans on a dirt road; he "felt that he could not take any prisoners," a unit report explained, "so he dispatched them."

Of the division's three parachute infantry regiments, only the 505th made a credible drop northwest of Ste.-Mère. A fire, perhaps ignited by a hissing flare, had awakened both the town and its German garrison. As a sexton hauled on the church bell-tower ropes, villagers passed canvas buckets hand over hand from the cattle-market pump to a blazing villa across the church square. Then, without warning, C-47s roared just overhead, wingtip to wingtip, spitting out paratroopers who frantically tugged on their risers to swerve away from both the flames and aroused German gunners.

A few GIs were butchered in their harnesses, including one young trooper who dangled from a tree bough "with eyes open, as though looking down at his own bullet holes," as the Ste.-Mère mayor recorded. But hundreds more landed unharmed after pilots circled back through the gunfire to find the correct drop zone. The 3rd Battalion commander, Lieutenant Colonel Edward C. Krause, known as Cannonball, managed to round up a quarter of his men. Led through the shadows by a drunk Frenchman as a guide, they crept into Ste.-Mère from the northwest, bounding between doorways with orders to avoid telltale muzzle flashes by using only knives, bayonets, and grenades. Ten Germans died defending the town they had held for four years, but most fled and a few hard sleepers were captured in their bunks. Four hundred yards from the church square, Krause personally severed the cable to Cherbourg. Patrols built

A U.S. paratrooper fires into a church steeple in Ste.-Mère Église to clear enemy snipers.

roadblocks outside town with antitank mines and plastic explosive Gammon grenades. A burial detail cut down a half-dozen dead paratroopers still dangling from the chestnut trees.

In front of the town hall, Krause pulled an American flag from his backpack and hoisted it on a wobbly pole. At five A.M. he sent a runner—few radios had survived the drop—with a message that reached the division commander, Major General Matthew B. Ridgway: "I am in Ste. Mère Église." An hour later a second runner carried a postscript: "I have secured Ste. Mère Église." The Americans had liberated their first town in France.

By dawn, 816 planes and 100 gliders had inserted more than 13,000 GIs onto the Continent; only 21 planes had been shot down, far less than the carnage predicted by Air Marshal

Leigh-Mallory. Yet only one of six regiments had been delivered where intended. Air commanders had not sent an advance weather plane to warn of the low cloud banks so common over Normandy in June; in this failure, they were remiss if not derelict. Dispersion thinned the combat power of a force armed with little more than rifles and grenades. But the haphazard scattering was "not an unmixed evil," as the official army history would put it: dispersion confused the enemy as well as the dispersed. Across the Cotentin Peninsula could be heard the metallic *thwang* of phone and telegraph wires snipped by Allied paratroopers. Captured Germans were ordered to lie on their backs in a circle, feet touching, awaiting evacuation to prisoner cages. Many others, gunned down in ambushes, simply lay dead.

Shortly before dawn, an American light bomber flew the first night photo-reconnaissance mission over Europe, illuminating the Norman landscape from 8,000 feet with a 200-million-candlepower electric lamp carried in the open bomb bay like a tiny sun. After shooting 180 photographs, the plane circled back to England, where analysts would study the film, frame by frame, looking for German panzer tanks trundling toward the Cotentin Peninsula in the inevitable German counterattack.

A reconnaissance photo taken over Normandy on the morning of D-Day. Gliders sit in the fields.

BRIDGES OVER THE ORNE AND AT CAEN

FIFTY MILES to the east, the British 6th Airborne Division had crossed the coast of France, eager to settle scores after half a decade of war. Tommies hoping to bop a sleeping German heaved miscellaneous objects out the open doors of their transport planes: bricks inscribed with vulgar words, a soccer ball painted to resemble Hitler's face, and a stuffed moose head stolen from an Exeter pub. Almost five thousand paratroopers and glidermen followed.

Two parachute brigades were to secure OVERLORD's left flank by seizing bridges over the river Orne and its canal northeast of Caen while blowing up spans across the river Dives, which flowed roughly parallel five miles farther east. Many of the hardships plaguing their American comrades in the Cotentin Peninsula bedeviled the British too: more than half the pathfinders tasked with setting up lights at the drop zones landed in the wrong place, their electronic beacons and signal lamps damaged, missing, or invisible from the air after being ill-sited amid tall wheat. Evasive maneuvering by pilots knocked some paratroopers off balance and delayed their jumps; in one flock of ninety-one planes, only seventeen dropped in the correct spot. An antiaircraft shell blew a major from the 3rd Brigade through a hole in his plane's fuselage. With a static line wrapped around his legs, he dangled beneath the aircraft for half an hour until he was reeled back into the bay. He returned to England and then, later that day, made France by glider, mussed but unharmed.

Less fortunate were the men dumped into the Atlantic or the flooded Dives Valley. One sodden brigadier took four hours to wade to the riverbank near Cabourg, steeping in the sixty

British Airborne Pathfinders check their watches on the night of June 5. Their helmets are camouflaged.

tea bags he had sewn into his uniform. "We could see where parachute canopies had collapsed in silken circles on the water," an officer reported. Bodies would be discovered in the Dives muck for the next half century.

Amid calamity came a celebrated success. Half a dozen large Horsa gliders, known as "Flying Morgues" for their tendency to disintegrate in hard landings, carried 181 men under Major John Howard, a former Oxford policeman. Cheered by urns of tea spiked with rum, they too had sung—"Cow Cow Boogie" and "It's a Long Way to Tipperary"—until the pilots shouted "Casting off!" and tow ropes parted from the Halifax bombers ahead. For three minutes Howard and his men sat in silence but for the shrieking wind, their arms linked and fingers locked. Three Horsas led by one called *Lady Irene* corkscrewed to the west until a pilot spotted their target and abruptly yelped, "Christ, there's the bridge!" Then: "Brace for impact!" With a sound likened by one private to "a giant sheet being ripped apart," the gliders clipped France at one hundred miles an hour, the wheels torn away as the Horsas bounded into the air, then settled down in an orange spray of sparks so intense the glidermen mistook them for German tracer bullets. Stunned but uninjured, Howard and his men wiggled headfirst through jagged holes in the glider fabric, lugging their guns and canvas buckets brimming with grenades.

There, hardly fifty yards from *Lady Irene*'s battered nose, stood the squat Bénouville bridge over a Caen canal. An astonished German sentry turned and fled, bellowing in alarm. A flare floated overhead, silvering the dark water, and fifty enemy soldiers stumbled toward the western bridge ramp as

A Horsa glider flipped onto its back while attempting to land in a pasture during the night of June 5–6. Troops killed in the crash are laid out on the grass.

gunfire pinged from girders and rails. Too late: Howard's men shot and grenaded their way across, shouting "Able," "Baker," and "Charlie" to keep the three platoons intact. "Anything that moved," a British soldier later acknowledged, "we shot."

One platoon commander fell dead from enemy fire, but within a quarter hour the span belonged to the British. The German bridge commander was captured when his car, laden with lingerie and perfume, skittered into a ditch; to atone for the loss of his honor, he asked in vain to be shot. Three rickety French tanks crewed by Germans lumbered toward the bridge only to be smacked with antiarmor fire. Two fled and the third burned for an hour after a crewman crawled from his hatch with both legs missing. Major Howard soon got word that the other half of his command had captured the nearby Orne River bridge at Ranville. He ordered the heartening news to be broadcast in a coded radio message, then dug in to await both reinforcement and a more resolute enemy counterstroke.

Across the Orne and Dives floodplains, additional gliders plummeted after midair collisions caused by treacherous crosswinds, or crash-landed with the usual mangled undercarriages. One Horsa skidded through a cottage and emerged, it was said, bearing a double bed with a French couple still under the duvet. Hunting horns and bugles tooted in the night as officers rallied their scattered companies. After one vicious burst of gunfire, an unhinged young paratrooper cried, "They got my mate! They got my mate!" Mates fell, but so did bridges: those over the Orne were captured, and four across the Dives were blown.

Perhaps the most perilous mission fell to the 9th Battalion of the Parachute Regiment, ordered to destroy a German coastal battery at Merville whose artillery was believed capable of reaching Sword Beach, easternmost of the five OVERLORD beaches. Surrounded by a cattle fence, minefields, barbed-wire thickets, and machine-gun pits, the big guns and two hundred gunners were protected by steel doors and concrete six feet thick, with twelve feet of dirt piled over the structure. Of 750 paratroopers dropped to do the deed, only 150 landed near the assembly area. Instead of sixty lengths of bangalore torpedo—metal tubes packed with explosive to tear barbed wire—just sixteen could be found by three A.M.

No matter. The bangalores blew two gaps rather than the planned four. Creeping paratroopers defused mines and trip-wired booby traps with their fingers. While a diversionary attack forced the main gate, assault teams slaughtered Germans by the score and disabled their guns. A signal officer dispatched the news to England by carrier pigeon. Though the guns proved both smaller and fewer than expected—only 75mm, and two rather than four—the menacing Merville battery had fallen. The price had been high: "I went in with 150," the battalion commander reported, "and came out with only 65 on their feet."

The toll had indeed been high for airborne forces on both flanks of the invasion crescent. Fewer than half of the 4,800 British troops now in France were either sufficiently near or sufficiently alive to join the fight in coherent units on June 6; still, the fraction exceeded that of American forces to the west. Yet this day would be famous even before it dawned, in no small measure because of the brave men who had come to war by air. Beset by mischance, confounded by disorder, they had mostly done what they were asked to do. Now the battle would hang on those who came by sea.

English Army troops release a carrier pigeon in this undated photo from World War II.

A British navy minesweeper on a practice run. The gun crew stands on a circular table that rotates as needed.

THE
BOMBERS

SHIP BY SHIP, convoy by convoy, the OVERLORD fleets slid into the broad, black Bay of the Seine. A vanguard of minesweepers carved an intricate maze of swept channels, marked by buoys agleam in the sea. Sailors and soldiers alike were astonished to find the Barfleur Lighthouse still burning east of Cherbourg; among the world's tallest and most conspicuous beacons, the rotating double flash was visible for thirty miles. Ahead lay the dark coastline, where it was said that Norman pirates once paraded lanterns on the horns of oxen to imitate ships' lights, pulling rings from the fingers of drowned passengers on vessels lured onto the reefs. Glints of gold and crimson could be seen far to starboard over the Cotentin Peninsula and far to port above the Orne River—airborne troops had apparently found the fight they were seeking. A pilot in a U.S. P-51 Mustang fighter-bomber, peering down at the armada spread across the

Barfleur Lighthouse

B-26 Marauder fighter bombers, made in the U.S., provide cover for D-Day landings.

teeming sea, would recognize an ancient secret: "War in these conditions is, for a short span, magnificent."

On the pitching decks of the ships, grandeur remained elusive. Riflemen on the bridge wings of two old Channel steamers, H.M.S. *Prince Baudouin* and H.M.S. *Prince Leopold*, watched for mines beyond the bow waves. A veteran sergeant from Virginia aboard the U.S.S. *Samuel Chase* recorded, "The waiting is always the worst. The mind can wander."

At two A.M. the ship's loudspeaker on *Samuel Chase* broke up a poker game and summoned GIs to breakfast, where mess boys in white jackets served pancakes and sausage. In lesser messes, troops picked at cold sandwiches or tinned beef. On the bridge of H.M.S. *Danae*, an officer shared out sips of "the most superb 1812 brandy from a bottle laid down by my great-grandfather in 1821."

U.S. troops and medical personnel wait for the moment of attack.

DECEPTION

PRECISELY WHAT the enemy knew about the approaching convoys remained uncertain. The German radar network—it stretched from Norway to Spain, with a major site every ten miles on the North Sea and English Channel coasts—had been bombed by the Allies for the past month. In recent days, 120 installations at 47 sites between Calais and Cherbourg had received particular attention from Allied fighter-bombers and the most intense electronic jamming ever unleashed; the German early-warning system had now been reduced to an estimated 5 percent of capacity. Various deceptions also played out, including the deployment of three dozen balloons with radar reflectors to simulate invasion ships where none sailed. Near Calais, where a German radar site had deliberately been left functioning, Allied planes dumped metal confetti, known as Window, into the airstream to mimic the electronic signature of bomber formations sweeping toward northern France.

West of Le Havre and Boulogne, planes flying meticulously calibrated oblong courses also scattered enough Window to simulate two large naval fleets, each covering two hundred square miles, steaming toward the coast at eight knots.

The actual OVERLORD fleets deployed an unprecedented level of electronic sophistication that foreshadowed twenty-first-century warfare. Six hundred and three jammers had been distributed to disrupt the search and fire-control radars operating from enemy fortifications, including 240 transmitters carried aboard LCTs and other small craft headed for the beaches, and 120 high-powered jammers to protect large warships. Jamming had begun at 9:30 P.M. on June 5, when the first ships drew within fifteen miles of that brilliant Barfleur light.

German bombers

Of particular concern were glide bombs, dropped from aircraft and guided by German pilots using a joystick and a radio transmitter. First used by the Luftwaffe, the German air force, in August 1943, glide bombs—notably a model called the Fritz-X—had sunk the Italian battleship *Roma* and nearly sank the cruiser U.S.S. *Savannah* off Salerno, Italy. Hitler had stockpiled Fritz-Xs and the similar Hs-293 to attack any invasion. The Allied Intelligence project, Ultra, revealed that 145 radio-control bombers now flew from French airports. The dozen different jammer variants humming in the Bay of the Seine included devices designed against glide bombs specifically. In cramped quarters on U.S.S. *Bayfield* and other ships, oscilloscope operators stared at their screens for the telltale electronic *pip, pip* of a glide bomb. After pinpointing the precise enemy frequency, a good countermeasures team could begin jamming within ten seconds. A successful jam would redirect the bomb from its target.

One part of the deception, called Operation FORTITUDE, was to place decoy tanks and guns near ports the Germans expected the Allies to use.

IT IS NOW
D-DAY

ALLIED BOMBING had intensified at midnight. "Each time they woke us up in the night somebody would say, 'It's D-Day.' But it never was," wrote Bert Stiles, an American B-17 pilot. "And then on the sixth of June it was." More than a thousand British heavy bombers struck coastal batteries and inland targets in the small hours, gouging gaping craters along the Norman seaboard. Antiaircraft fire rose like a white curtain, and flames licked from damaged Allied planes laboring back toward the Channel. Transfixed men aboard U.S.S. *Augusta* watched a stricken bomber with all four engines streaming fire plunge directly at the ship before swerving to starboard to crash amid the waves a mile away.

Behind the British came virtually the entire American bomber fleet of 1,635 planes. B-26 Marauder crews, aware that paratroopers in the Cotentin Peninsula were pressing toward the causeways on the peninsula's eastern lip, flew parallel to the shoreline below six thousand feet to drop 4,414 bombs with commendable accuracy along Utah Beach.

Less precise was the main American force, the 1,350 B-17 Flying Fortresses and B-24 Liberators of the Eighth Air Force, flying from England in a roaring corridor ten miles wide and led by pathfinder planes tossing out flares at one-mile intervals like burning bread crumbs. Their targets included forty-five coastal fortifications, mostly within rifle range of the high-water mark from Sword Beach in the east to Omaha in the west. Given the imprecision of heavy bombers at sixteen thousand feet—under perfect conditions, less than half their bombs were likely to fall within a quarter mile of an aim point—the primary intent was not to pulverize enemy defenses but to demoralize German defenders beneath the weight of metal.

Conditions were far from perfect. Clouds shrouded the coast as the formations arrived over land, six squadrons abreast on a course perpendicular to the beaches. Eisenhower a week earlier had agreed to permit clumsy "blind bombing" if necessary, using radar to pick out the shoreline and approximate target locations. On the night of June 5, he authorized another abrupt change requested by Eighth Air Force: to avoid accidentally hitting the approaching invasion flotillas, bombardiers would delay dumping their weapons for an additional five to thirty seconds beyond the normal release point.

For an hour and a half, three thousand tons of bombs gouged the Norman landscape. Minefields, phone wires, and rocket pits inland were obliterated, but less than 2 percent of all bombs fell in the assault areas, and virtually none hit the shoreline or beach fortifications. Repeated warnings against killing their own troops "had the effect of producing an over-cautious attitude in the minds of most of the bombardiers," an Eighth Air Force analysis later concluded; some added "many seconds" to the half-minute "bombs away" delay already imposed. Nearly all payloads tumbled a mile or two from the coast, and some fell farther. Many thousands of bombs were wasted: no defenders had been ejected from their concrete lairs. Whether they felt demoralized by the flame and apocalyptic noise behind them would be discerned only when the first invasion troops touched shore.

Bombs being loaded into a U.S. B-17 Flying Fortress.

MORE
SHIPS THAN SEA

HEAVY CHAINS RATTLED across the bay, followed by splash after mighty splash as anchors slapped the sea and sank from sight. An anguished voice cried from a darkened deck, "For Chrissake, why in the hell don't we send the Krauts a telegram and let them know we're here?" Another voice called out: "Anchor holding, sir, in seventeen fathoms."

Aboard *Princess Astrid*, six miles from Sword Beach, a loudspeaker summons—"Troops to parade, troops to parade"— brought assault platoons to the deck. On ships eleven miles off Omaha, GIs in the 116th Infantry pushed single file through double blackout curtains to climb to the top decks. Landing craft, described as "oversized metal shoeboxes," swung from cranes, waiting to be loaded with soldiers; others would be lowered empty, smacking against the steel hulls, to be boarded by GIs creeping down the cargo nets that sailors now spread over the sides. A Coast Guard lieutenant on *Bayfield* watched troops "adjusting their packs, fitting bayonets to their rifles and puffing on cigarettes as if that would be their last. There was complete silence." Scribbling in his diary he added, "One has the feeling of approaching a great abyss."

On June 6 at 5:16 A.M. in Normandy, the ascending sun was twelve degrees below the eastern horizon. For the next forty-two minutes, until sunrise at 5:58, the dawning day revealed what enemy radar had not. To a German soldier near Vierville, the fleet materialized "like a gigantic town" afloat, while a French boy peering from his window in Grandcamp saw "more ships than sea."

Minesweepers nosed close to shore, clearing lanes for 140 warships preparing to drench the coast with gunfire. Blinkered messages from minesweepers just two miles off the

A convoy of LCIs sails toward Normandy, each towing a barrage balloon.

British beaches of Gold, Juno, and Sword reported no hint of enemy stirrings, and Omaha Beach too appeared placid. But at 5:30 A.M., on the approaches to Utah Beach, black splashes abruptly leaped mast-high in the front and back of the cruisers H.M.S. *Black Prince* and U.S.S. *Quincy*, followed by the distant bark of shore guns. Two destroyers also took fire three miles from the beach, and a minesweeper fled out to sea, chased by large shells coming from St.-Vaast. At 5:36 A.M., after allowing Mustang and Spitfire spotter planes time to pinpoint German muzzle flashes, Rear Admiral Deyo ordered, "Commence counterbattery bombardment."

Soon enough, eight hundred naval guns thundered along a fifty-mile firing line. Sailors packed cotton in their ears. "The

The U.S.S. Arkansas *covers the beaches with its 12-inch guns.*

air vibrated," wrote the reporter Don Whitehead. Shells thumped heavily as they dropped into loading trays before being rammed into the breech. Gun turrets turned landward. Two sharp buzzes signaled *Stand by*, then a single buzz for *Fire!* "Clouds of yellow . . . smoke billowed up," wrote A. J. Liebling as he watched the battleship *Arkansas* from *LCI-88*. The 12- and 14-inch shells from the battleships *Arkansas* and *Texas* sounded "like railway trains thrown skyward," wrote Ernest Hemingway, watching through binoculars as a war correspondent aboard H.M.S. *Empire Anvil*. Paint peeled from *Nevada*'s scorched gun barrels, baring blue steel, and sailors swept cork shell casings and the burned silk from powder bags into the sea. David K. E. Bruce, an Office of Strategic Services operative who would later serve as U.S. ambassador in three European capitals, wrote in his diary aboard U.S.S. *Tuscaloosa*:

> *There is cannonading on all sides as well as from the shore. . . . The air is acrid with powder, and a fine spray of disintegrated wadding comes down on us like lava ash. . . . The deck trembles under our feet, and the joints of the ship seem to creak and stretch. . . . Repeated concussions have driven the screws out of their sockets [and] shattered light bulbs.*

German shells soared over the bay in crimson curves. "The arc at its zenith looks as if it would end up on the *Quincy*," wrote an officer eyeing an approaching round. "I am wrong, happily wrong." Ships zigged, zagged, and zigged some more, their battle flags snapping and their wakes boiling white. Seasoned sailors could gauge the size of an enemy shell from the

German soldiers aim toward the invading Allies.

height of the splash, including the 210mm ship-killers shot from the three-gun battery at St.-Marcouf. "It is a terrible and monstrous thing to have to fire on our homeland," an admiral on the French cruiser *Montcalm* advised his crew, "but I want you to do it this day." A French woman ashore wrote in her diary, "It is raining iron. The windows are exploding, the floor is shaking, we are choking in the smell of gunpowder." She piled her children and mattresses onto a horse cart and fled inland.

Experience from the battles in the Pacific suggested that naval bombardment against strong coastal defenses should last days, even weeks. But profound differences existed between battering an isolated island and shelling from the shallow, cramped English Channel, a long coastline with interior roads that permitted quick enemy reinforcement. The job was tougher because German gun casemates had concrete walls and ceilings up to twelve feet thick. Consequently the preparatory bombardment for the American beaches in OVER-LORD lasted barely half an hour in order to get on with the landings. Allied ships on June 6 fired 140,000 shells, but few enemy fortifications were destroyed. Of 218 huge shells and almost 1,000 6-inch rounds flung at the battery at Houlgate, for example, only one direct hit was recorded. Of 28 batteries capable of reaching Utah Beach with 111 guns, none were completely knocked out in the dawn barrage. And despite being hammered by three battleships, a heavy cruiser, and other lesser vessels, that pesky St.-Marcouf battery would hold out until June 12. As with the air bombardment, the extent to which German defenders were unmanned by the naval pummeling would be revealed only by making land.

The 14-inch guns on the U.S.S. Nevada *in action on the morning of June 6.*

UTAH: "HOW DO YOU BOYS LIKE THE BEACH?"

This photo of Brigadier General Theodore Roosevelt, Jr., was taken during the Sicily campaign in 1943. His jeep, Rough Rider, is named after the volunteer regiment he organized for service in the Spanish-American War.

BRIGADIER GENERAL ROOSEVELT intended to see with his own congenitally weak, vaguely crossed eyes just how strong the enemy defenses remained.

The Channel's typical tidal flow required staggering the five beach landings over the space of an hour; Utah, the westernmost, would be first, and Roosevelt would be first among the first, landing with the initial twenty assault boats of the 4th Infantry Division. After a peevish exchange aboard U.S.S. *Barnett* over his missing life belt—"I've already given you three," an exasperated aide complained—he stumped to the ship's wet rail, patting his shoulder holster. "I've got my pistol, one clip of ammunition, and my walking cane," he announced in his foghorn bass. "That's all I expect to need." When a soldier leaned across from the dangling landing craft to offer a hand, Roosevelt swatted it aside. "Get the hell out of my way. I can jump in there by myself. You know I can take it as well as any of you." Springing five feet into the boat, he steadied himself with his cane as the craft was lowered into the heaving waves. Sailors cast off as Roosevelt bantered with the pale, wide-eyed men around him because, as he had written Eleanor, "there are shadows when they stop to think."

"Away all boats," a voice called from above. Icy water sloshed around the ankles of thirty soldiers, already shivering and vomiting, packed like sardines in the thirty-six-foot hull. A coxswain gunned the diesel engine, swinging the blunt bow into the swell, and Ted Roosevelt headed back to the war.

At 6:30 A.M., the boat ramp dropped one hundred yards from shore. Drenched, cold, and exhilarated, Roosevelt waded waist-deep through the surf and onto France.

He was on the wrong beach. Billowing dust from the air and naval bombardment hid what few landmarks existed on the flat coastline, and the two guide boats leading the flotilla had fallen back—one with a fouled propeller, the other sunk with a hole in the port bow from a mine. Rather than landing adjacent to the causeway over the flooded marshlands, Roosevelt and his spearhead

U.S. soldiers wait to board landing craft to Utah Beach. Waterproof bags cover their guns.

An aerial view of soldiers and landing craft surging onto Utah Beach, photographed from an air force bomber.

of six hundred men had come ashore almost two thousand yards south. Worse still, eight LCTs carrying thirty-two Sherman tanks, outfitted with propellers and inflatable canvas bloomers allowing them to putter to shore, had been delayed when one vessel tripped another mine. Four tanks went to the bottom and some twenty men to their graves. Rather than beaching just behind the assault infantry as intended, the remaining Shermans would arrive twenty minutes late.

Weak eyes or no, Roosevelt recognized his plight. Hobbling into the dunes, he spied a windmill and other structures far to the north. "We're not where we're supposed to be," he told the 8th Infantry commander, Colonel James A. Van Fleet, who arrived at seven A.M. "You see that brick building over there to our right front? It always showed up in those aerial photographs, and it was always on the left. . . . I'm sure we're about a mile or two miles farther south."

The accidental beach proved pleasingly benign, with few fortifications, fewer vertical wooden beach obstacles, and little enemy artillery; German defenders there did indeed seem dazed by the air and naval pummeling. Wave followed wave of landing craft, jammed with standing troops. Roosevelt worked the waterline "with a cane in one hand, a map in the other, walking around as if he was looking over some real estate," as one sergeant recalled. Occasional enemy shells detonated in the dunes with a concussion likened by Hemingway to "a punch with a heavy, dry glove." Few of the shells fell with precision.

"How do you boys like the beach?" Roosevelt roared at arriving 12th Infantry troops. "It's a great day for hunting. Glad you made it!" Engineers swarmed ashore, blowing beach obstacles and gaps in the masonry seawall with "Hell Box" charges and cries of "Fire in the hole!" Demolition teams had hoped to clear the beaches in twelve hours; instead, ninety minutes after Roosevelt first sloshed ashore, the fleet was advised that all boats could land with "no fear of impaling themselves on the obstacles."

Through the dunes and across the beach road, several thousand GIs—the first of 32,000 in Force U—cleared resistance nests with grenades, submachine guns, and tank fire. Four causeways leading to the interior would be seized on June 6, including one under a foot of water. To avoid clogging the narrow roads, swimmers and nonswimmers from the 12th Infantry paired off to cross the flooded fields. "I gave an arm signal," the regimental commander reported, "and three thousand heavily burdened infantrymen walked into the man-made lake."

The mutter of gunfire sounded along a three-mile front, scarlet tracers skipping like hot stones across the water. Soldiers waggled swatches of orange signal cloth, peering westward through the haze for answering waggles from the 101st Airborne. In the far south, a tank lieutenant hopped down from his Sherman tank to help a wounded paratrooper only to trip a mine, blowing off both of his feet; his crew dragged both damaged men to safety with ropes. A dead German soldier was found stripped to the waist, shaving cream still on his chin. Other Germans were mowed down or captured, including fifty gunners with three horse-drawn 88mm guns. An enemy soldier burned by a flamethrower was evacuated to the beach, charred and blistered but still breathing. "It sure takes a lot to kill a German," a Coast Guard lieutenant told his diary. GIs snipped the unit patches from enemy sleeves and gave them to intelligence analysts.

East of Pouppeville, a 101st Airborne squad cautiously summoned scouts from the 4th Division across the causeway. "Where's the war?" an 8th Infantry soldier asked, rifle slung on his shoulder. A paratrooper gestured vaguely inland. "Anywhere from here on back." Soon enough Roosevelt raced up in his newly landed jeep, *Rough Rider*. Hearing the slap of artillery ahead, he shouted to an officer, "Hey, boy, they're shooting up there," then cackled with laughter as he drove off to the sound of the guns.

Eleven miles offshore, aboard U.S.S. *Bayfield*, the naval commander of Force U, Rear Admiral Don P. Moon, sent a heartening battle report at 9:45 A.M.: fifteen of twenty-six waves landed; obstacles cleared; vehicles moving inland. Moon's buoyant dispatch belied a fretful anxiety: the loss of vessels had already led him to delay seven assault waves, and now he had all but decided to halt the landings completely until minesweepers could carefully comb the shallows.

In his spare office aboard *Bayfield*, Moon revealed his plan to halt the landings to Major General J. Lawton Collins, the Army's VII Corps commander. He would oversee all operations in the Cotentin Peninsula once Force U reached shore.

The U.S. 9th Infantry dug in at the seawall on Utah Beach.

Collins ticked off the reasons to continue to press ahead: light resistance on Utah Beach, with fewer than two hundred casualties in the 4th Division; troops boring inland; naval losses painful but moderate. More to the point, the 101st Airborne needed urgent reinforcement, and nothing had been heard from the 82nd Airborne. "I had to put my foot down hard to persuade the admiral," Collins later said.

Persuade him he did. Moon relented, with misgivings, then assumed a brave face in a brief, stilted statement to news reporters on his flagship. "It is our good fortune, which always goes with parties who plan well, that Force U has made a successful landing," he told them, then added, "The initial action has been won."

Enemy fire at Utah Beach.

OMAHA: HELL'S BEACH

U.S. troops approach Omaha Beach.

FIFTEEN MILES SOUTHEAST of Utah was a sea-chewed plateau named La Côte du Calvados. In various Allied plans, the crescent beach below the bluffs had been labeled Beach 46, Beach 313, and X Beach; now it was known as Omaha. Five miles long, composed of packed sand yielding to pebbles, the beach offered only five exits up the hundred-foot cliff, each following a narrow watercourse to four villages of thick-walled farmhouses a mile or so inland. June airs usually came from the south, but on this morning the wind whistled from the northwest at almost twenty knots, accelerating the current from two knots to three, which ran easterly or westerly depending on the tide.

That Norman tide was a primordial force unseen in any previous amphibious landing. Rising twenty-three feet, twice daily it inundated the beach and everything on it at a rate of a vertical foot every eight minutes, then ebbed at almost an inch per second. Low tide typically revealed four hundred yards of open beach, but six hours later that low-tide mark would lie more than twenty feet deep. To finesse this phenomenon in landing the 30,000 assault troops of Task Force O, followed by 26,000 more in Force B, planners chose to attack on a rising tide the morning of June 6. This would permit landing craft to ferry the assault force as far up the exposed beach as possible, but without stranding the boats as the tide retreated. Ten thousand combat engineers would land with the infantry on June 6, as the historian Joseph Balkoski has written, yet the first demolitions experts, known as sappers, would have only half an hour to blow open lanes among the beach obstacles for landing craft before the rising sea hid the vicious metal spikes.

OVERLORD's plan called for nine infantry companies to attack simultaneously on the beach that had been divided into segments: Charlie, Dog, Easy, and Fox. But three mistakes had already given Omaha a tragic cast—one error attributable mostly to the navy, two to the army. To minimize the risk of German shore fire, naval captains had anchored their transport ships eleven miles distant, guaranteeing confused landings because of wind and current. In a bid for tactical surprise, army commanders had insisted on reducing the naval bombardment to barely thirty-five minutes—enough to scare the defenders but not enough, given the clean miss by Allied air forces, to subdue them. The army had also chosen to storm the narrow beach exits where fortifications were sturdiest, rather than infiltrating up the bluffs to outflank enemy strong points.

The German defenses were fearsome. Eighty-five machine-gun nests, soon known to GIs as "murder holes," covered

This photo was taken from a Coast Guard barge landing soldiers on Easy Red. In front are two landing craft from the U.S.S. Samuel Chase.

Omaha, more than all three British beaches combined. Unlike the obstacles at Utah, many of the 3,700 wood pilings and iron barriers embedded in the tidal flat at Omaha were draped with mines. Thirty-five dug-in concrete machine-gun posts, called pillboxes, and eight massive bunkers—some "as big as a New England town hall," in one reporter's description—defended the beach's five exits, while eighteen antitank sites, six rocket-launcher pits, and four artillery positions covered the balance of the beach. Guns raked nearly every grain of sand on Omaha, concealed from the sea by concrete and earthen blast shields that aerial photos had failed to find. Thanks to smokeless, flashless powder and a German ban on tracer bullets here, gun pits remained, as a navy analysis conceded, "exceedingly difficult to detect."

Also undetected and unexpected by the assault troops were German reinforcements. German field marshal Erwin Rommel in mid-March had shifted the 352nd Infantry Division to the coast from St.-Lô, twenty miles inland, placing two regiments behind Omaha and Gold Beaches alongside two regiments from the feebler 716th Infantry Division. In addition, a third 352nd regiment bivouacked in reserve at Bayeux. Neither Ultra nor conventional intelligence sniffed out the move; belated suspicions of reinforcement reached Omar Bradley's First Army headquarters on June 4, too late to alert the scattered fleets under a radio blackout. The thirteen thousand troops from the German 352nd—mobile, dangerous, and

Medics on Fox Green give a plasma transfusion to a survivor of a landing craft attack.

Injured soldiers on Omaha Beach.

so young that officers requisitioned milk from French farmers to build their bones—had spent much of their time in recent weeks hauling timber in carts from the Cerisy Forest to support the Atlantic Wall. The Omaha defenses remained far more lethal than the single immobile regiment scattered over a fifty-mile front that most GIs had expected to knock aside. Rather than the three-to-one ratio favored by attackers in storming an entrenched foe, some units now sweeping toward land would meet odds of three to five. The beach that had first warranted only a succession of code numbers, and then a homely code name, now would earn other enduring epithets, including Bloody Omaha and Hell's Beach.

For those who outlived the day, the memories would remain as shot-torn as the beach itself. They remembered waves slapping the steel hulls, and bilge pumps choked with vomit from seasick men making "utterly inhuman noises." Green water curled over the gunwales as coxswains waited for a tidal surge to lift them past the sandbars before dropping the ramps with a heavy *clank* and a shouted benediction: "It's yours, take it away!"

They remembered the red splash of shell bursts and machine-gun bullets puckering the sea "like wind-driven hail" before tearing through the grounded boats so that, as one sergeant recalled, "men were tumbling out just like corn cobs off a conveyor belt." Mortar fragments said to be the size of shovel blades skimmed the shore, trimming away arms, legs, heads. The murder holes murdered. Steel-jacketed rounds kicked up sand "like wicked living things," as a reporter wrote, or swarmed overhead in what Vernon Scannell called an "insectile whine." Soldiers who had sung "Happy D-Day, dear Adolf" now cowered like frightened animals. They desperately gouged out shallow holes in the sand with mess kit spoons and bare knuckles, mouths held open in astonishment and to prevent artillery concussions from rupturing their eardrums.

Army and navy engineers, lugging twenty-eight tons of explosives, were supposed to land three minutes behind the infantry spearhead to blow sixteen gaps, each fifty yards wide, through tidal-zone obstacles. Little went right: some engineers landed early and alone, some landed late, nearly all drifted left—east—of their assigned beaches by up to a mile because of the current and navigation error. An 88mm shell hit Team 14's landing craft, blowing the coxswain overboard and slaughtering the vessel's entire navy demolition squad.

A U.S. Coast Guard boat rescues two survivors off Normandy after their ship was hit.

Seven died in Team 11 when shellfire hit their rubber boat; of forty men in Team 15, only four eluded death or injury. A mortar round caught Team 12, tripping the TNT detonating cord and explosive charges and killing or wounding nineteen engineers in a violent explosion.

Demolitionists shinnied up pilings or stood on one another's shoulders to pluck off mines and place their charges, popping violet smoke grenades to signal an imminent detonation. Gunfire shot away fuses as fast as engineers could rig them, including one burst that also carried off the fuse man's fingers. Terrified infantrymen sheltered behind the German obstacles "like a cluster of bees," even as engineers screamed, kicked, and threatened to blow their charges anyway. By seven A.M., as the floodtide began to swallow the obstacles, only six of sixteen gaps had been cleared, and at an awful cost: more than half of the engineers would be dead, wounded, or missing by midmorning.

The failures multiplied. Sherman amphibious tanks, ostensibly seagoing with their inflatable canvas skirts and twin propellers, began plopping into the waves from LCT ramps "like toads from the lip of an ornamental pond," as the historian John Keegan later wrote. Of thirty-two Shermans in one battalion, twenty-seven sank trying to cross six thousand yards of open water, with a loss of 146 men. Farther west, a navy lieutenant sensibly recognized the rough sea as unfit for a thirty-three-ton swimming tank, and LCTs carrying most of another armored battalion made for shore instead. Eight Shermans went under when their vessels took direct hits, but twenty-four others clanked ashore.

Sherman tanks drive off a landing craft.

Artillerymen also struggled to land their guns. A dozen 105mm howitzers from the 111th Field Artillery Battalion had been loaded onto amphibious trucks known as DUKWs or

A DUKW, or "Duck," a six-wheel-drive amphibious truck.

"Ducks," each of which also carried fourteen men and fifty shells and was encased in eighteen sandbags for protection— enough weight to make the DUKW "altogether unseaworthy," as the army belatedly recognized. Eight quickly took on water and capsized, and three others were lost to waves or shellfire before reaching shore.

Two infantry regiments washed onto Hell's Beach early that morning from the two assault divisions that formed V Corps. To the west was the 116th Infantry from Virginia, who had trained in Britain for twenty months. Officers ordered men in landing craft approaching the shore to keep their heads down, as one lieutenant explained, "so they wouldn't see it and lose heart." They saw soon enough. On the right flank of the invasion zone, German gunners abruptly turned beach Dog Green into a slaughterhouse. Without firing a shot, Company A was reportedly "inert and leaderless" in ten minutes; after half an hour, two-thirds of the company had been destroyed, including Sergeant Frank Draper, Jr., killed when an antitank round tore away his left shoulder to expose a heart that beat until he bled to death. Among twenty-two men from tiny Bedford, Virginia, who would die in Normandy, Draper "didn't get to kill anybody," his sister later lamented. A surviving officer reported that his men fell "like hay dropping before the scythe."

German machine guns—with a sound one GI compared to "a venetian blind being lifted up rapidly"—perforated the beach, killing the wounded and rekilling the dead. All thirty-two soldiers in one boat, *LCA-1015*, were slaughtered, including their captain. A lieutenant shot in the brain continued to direct his troops until, a survivor recounted, "he sat down and held his head in the palm of his hand before falling over dead." Wounded men jabbed themselves with morphine or shrieked for medics, one of whom used safety pins to close a gaping leg wound. "A guy in front of me got it through the throat. Another guy in front of me got it through the heart," a survivor later recalled. An unhinged soldier sat in the sand, weeping softly and tossing stones into the water. "This," an officer declared, "is a debacle."

BETWEEN EASY RED
AND FOX GREEN

MORE THAN A MILE to the east, the 16th Infantry Regiment had its own debacle. The entire first wave landed east of its intended beaches. Simply reaching the waterline reduced Company L from 187 men to 123. Medics found that "the greater portion of the dead had died of bullet wounds through the head"; officers and sergeants alike began slapping wet sand over the rank insignia on their helmets to confound snipers. "Fire was coming from everywhere, big and little stuff," a soldier in Company E recalled. One sergeant calculated that the beach was swept with "at least twenty thousand bullets and shells per minute." Robert Capa, who had removed his Contax camera from its waterproof oilskin to snap the most memorable photographs of the Second World War, crouched behind a burned-out Sherman tank on Easy Red and murmured a phrase he recalled from the Spanish Civil War: "*Es una cosa muy seria.*" "This is a very serious business."

The four-hundred-ton *LCI-85*, grounding ashore on the seam between Easy Red and Fox Green, had begun dispensing men down the left ramp when enemy 47mm and 88mm shells blew through the front hold, killing fifteen and wounding forty-seven. The coast guard crew backed off and steamed west several hundred yards, only to face scorching fire upon trying again. More than two dozen shells ripped into the ship, igniting troop compartments and leaving the decks slick with blood. On the bridge, the skipper reported, "We could hear the screams of the men through the voice tube." Listing, burning, bleeding, *LCI-85* steamed for the horizon, where the wounded and the dead were extracted before she capsized and sank.

By 8:30 A.M. the Omaha assault had stalled. The rising tide quickly reclaimed the thin strip of liberated beach, drowning those immobilized by wounds or fear. With no room to land more vehicles, a navy beachmaster halted further unloading

The first wave of American troops cling to beach obstacles to protect themselves from enemy fire at Omaha Beach. This photograph was taken by Robert Capa.

Swimming ashore. This photograph was taken by Robert Capa.

on much of the shoreline. "Face downwards, as far as eyes could see in either direction," a 16th Infantry surgeon later wrote, "were the huddled bodies of men living, wounded, and dead, as tightly packed together as layers of cigars in a box."

Two large boats burned furiously in the shallows of Dog White. *LCI-91*, carrying two hundred soldiers, had caught a shell in her fuel tanks, engulfing part of the deck in flames. At least two dozen men were incinerated as others leaped into the sea, including one who dove in with even the soles of his boots blazing. Moments later, *LCI-92*, seeking cover in her sister's smoke, struck a mine on the port bow. "A sheet of flame shot up thirty feet in the air," a soldier reported. "Terror seized me." German gunners then finished off the boat. A survivor dog-paddled to the beach not as an infantry officer ready for combat, as he later acknowledged, but as the "helpless unarmed survivor of a shipwreck."

FOUR MILES WEST
OF OMAHA

ON THE CLIFFS four miles west of Omaha, the early-morning assault showed promise. Three companies from the 2nd Ranger Battalion scaled the headland at Pointe du Hoc, first climbing freehand despite a rain of grenades, then using hooks and braided ropes fired from mortar tubes. Comrades gave covering fire from ladders loaned by the London Fire Department and carried in DUKWs. The top of the cliff had been reduced to what one officer called "ripped-open dirt" by 250 shells from *Texas*'s 14-inch barrels. Rangers hauled themselves over the lip of the cliff, then used grenades to wreck five shore guns that had been removed from their casemates and hidden in an apple orchard. The triumph was short-lived: they soon found themselves trapped by rallying Germans who spent the next thirty-six hours trying to sweep them from the cliff to the rocks below.

Back on Hell's Beach, several thousand shivering soldiers

found protection where they could and waited for a counter-attack from the bluffs to bowl them back into the sea. "They'll come swarming down on us," murmured journalist Don Whitehead. A lieutenant who watched sodden bodies advance on the creeping tide later wrote, "After a couple of looks back, we decided we couldn't look back anymore." Among those huddled on the beach was Captain Joseph T. Dawson, a lanky, dark-eyed veteran of Company G in the 16th Infantry. An hour earlier, Dawson had leaped from his landing craft onto Easy Red just as an artillery shell struck the boat, killing the thirty-three men behind him. "The limitations of life come into sharp relief," he would write his family in Texas. "No one is indispensable in this world."

U.S. Rangers, using a rope ladder, climb a cliff at Pointe du Hoc.

ON THE
COMMAND SHIP

FROM THE GRAY DECK of the command ship U.S.S. *Augusta*, none of this was clear. A brown fog of dust and smoke draped the French coast to the south, mysterious and impenetrable except by the cherry-red battleship shells soaring toward inland targets. A cramped First Army war room had been built on the cruiser's afterdeck, ten feet by twenty, with a tarpaulin door, a map of France fastened to a sheet-metal wall, and a clock whose glass face had been criss-crossed with tape against breakage. Other maps displayed the suspected location

Landing craft speed toward the beach from the cruiser U.S.S. Augusta.

of enemy units, marked in red, and the range of German shore guns, shown by concentric circles. Signalmen wearing headphones listened for radio messages, which they pounded out on a bank of typewriters. From Omaha Beach only incoherent fragments had been heard, of sinkings, swampings, heavy fire. One dispatch picked up by another ship nearby advised, "We are being butchered like a bunch of hogs."

At a plotting table in the center of the war room sat a tall, bespectacled man in a helmet, life jacket, and three-star field jacket. Again he asked—"What's going on?"—and again got little more than an apologetic shrug. Omar Bradley knew from studying military history that the most important accomplishment was "to get ground quickly." Was that happening at Omaha? Another shrug. He had expected the two assault regiments to be a mile inland by 8:30 A.M., but now he was unsure whether they had even reached France. Bradley had begun contemplating his course if the troops failed to get off the beach.

After successfully commanding a corps in Africa and Sicily, Bradley had benefited from adoring press coverage, including a recent *Time* magazine cover story that called him "Lincolnesque . . . a plain, homely, steady man with brains and character."

The Omaha plan had been largely Bradley's design, including the limited fire support from the navy, and he had dismissed predictions of stiff losses as "tommyrot."

Now he was not so sure. Messages from the beachhead remained fragmentary. "Obstacles mined, progress slow," said one. An aide dispatched by a patrol torpedo (PT) boat returned

American generals Omar N. Bradley and George S. Patton later in the war.

drenched and discouraged an hour later to report that troops were pinned down; a naval officer came back with a more vivid assessment: "My God, this is carnage!" Told that Rear Admiral Moon was jittery over ship losses, Bradley advised J. Lawton Collins, his VII Corps commander, "We've got to get the buildup ashore even if it means paving the whole damned Channel bottom with ships." Another 25,000 troops and 4,000 vehicles were scheduled to land at Omaha as the second invasion tide. Should these be diverted to Utah or to the British beaches? Would that leave those now ashore to be annihilated?

The man described in his high school yearbook as "calculative" pushed through the canvas war-room door and climbed to *Augusta*'s bridge, squinting at the opaque shore and mulling his odds.

GOOD NEWS AT DOG WHITE

NOT FOR SOME HOURS would Bradley learn that by late morning his prospects on Omaha had brightened considerably, beginning at beach Dog White. There Brigadier General "Dutch" Cota had reached the five-foot timber seawall half a mile east of the beach exit leading to Vierville. Soldiers who could outcrawl the tide lay clustered like barnacles on the wooden beams that jutted from the seawall.

We must improvise, carry on, not lose our heads, Cota had told officers from the 116th Infantry as they sailed for Normandy. Now he improvised. Chewing an unlit cigar, Cota scrabbled west along the beams. Pistol in hand, he sang tuneless, ad-libbed lyrics under his breath. Encountering a cluster of troops, he demanded, "What outfit is this? Goddamn it, if you're Rangers get up and lead the way. . . . I know you won't let me down. . . . We've got to get these men off this goddamned beach." A torpedo threaded through a double apron of barbed

Soldiers of the 116th Infantry repel enemy fire near Vierville on June 6.

wire blew a gap across the beach road beyond the seawall. Machine-gun fire cut down the first GI into the breach— "Medico, I'm hit," he cried, then sobbed for his mother until he died—but others, including Cota, scampered across the black-top and through the burning marsh grass beyond.

Up the bluff they climbed, single file, marking mines with white engineer tape, cigarettes, and scraps from a ration box. Smoke hid them from German marksmen but made them weep until they strapped on gas masks. Mortar rounds killed a trio of soldiers next to Cota and wounded his radioman; knocked flat but unscratched, the general regained his feet and followed the snaking column toward the top of the hill, past captured Germans spread-eagled on the ground. Then over the lip of the ridge they ran, past stunted pines and through uncut wheat as Cota yelled, "Now let's see what you're made of!" GIs hauling a captured MG-42 machine gun with ammunition belts draped around their necks poured fire into enemy trenches and at the broken enemy ranks running inland.

By ten A.M. tiny Vierville had fallen but for snipers. Terrified civilians peeked from their windows onto a road clogged with rubble. Another rifle company slipping into the village found Cota twirling his pistol on his finger. "Where the hell have you been, boys?" he asked.

Elsewhere along Omaha, in what one witness called "a final stubborn reserve of human courage," more desperate men found additional seams up the cliffs. "I walked slowly," a 29th Division soldier recalled, "dragging my unwilling soul with me." Halfway up the slope, a soldier missing a lower leg

Blowing barbed wire fences.

sat smoking a cigarette and fiddling with the tourniquet tied at his knee. "Watch it," he warned. "There are some personnel mines here." Captain Joe Dawson's G Company used GI corpses as stepping stones through a minefield. "Fire everywhere it seems," a major scribbled on an envelope used as a diary. "Prayed several times."

A dozen support destroyers—some so close to the beach that their keels scraped bottom—fired onto targets marked by army tracer and tank rounds. One soldier watching shells arc across the bluff reported that "a man standing there felt as if he could reach up and pick them out of the air." When a German artillery observer was spotted in the eleventh-century Colleville church tower, U.S.S. *Emmons* took a dozen rounds to find the range, then with the thirteenth knocked the tower into the main building and attached graveyard. A similar call for fire against the church of St.-Laurent shattered the steeple with the first shell. After one shuddering broadside from *Texas*, a Royal Air Force pilot spotting for the battleship cried from his Spitfire cockpit, "Oh, simply champion!"

French citizens fly their flag in a liberated town.

"THINGS LOOK BETTER"

BY NOON the enemy line had been broken by half a dozen penetrations. Two fresh regiments, the 115th Infantry and the 18th Infantry, swarmed over Easy Red before the ebb tide. Later the 26th Infantry also was ordered to shore. By midafternoon, some five thousand infantrymen had scaled the bluff. Scraps of news reached the fleet, including a message dispatched from a colonel in a DUKW: "Men believed ours on skyline. . . . Things look better." But only after one P.M. did Omar

American reinforcements disembark from a landing craft.

Bradley, pacing on *Augusta*'s flag bridge, learn in a message from V Corps that the day was saved, if not won: "Troops formerly pinned down on beaches Easy Red, Easy Green, Fox Red advancing up heights behind beaches."

Cota continued his charmed day by hiking from Vierville down the narrow ravine toward Dog Green, forcing five prisoners yanked from foxholes to guide him through a minefield. In a great geyser of masonry, engineers on the beach flats used a thousand pounds of dynamite to demolish a long anti-tank wall nine feet high and six feet thick. Armored bulldozers scraped debris from the Vierville gully, thus creating another opening for tanks, trucks, and the massive mechanized force that would be needed to liberate first Normandy, then France, then the continent beyond.

A German bunker built into the cliffs along Normandy beaches.

THE EASTERN FLANK:
GOLD, JUNO, AND SWORD

THAT LEFT THE BRITISH and Canadians, beating for three beaches to the east. Several tactical modifications aided the trio of assault divisions in Second Army: landing craft were launched seven miles from shore rather than the eleven typical in the American sector; the Royal Navy's bombardment lasted four times longer than that of the U.S. Navy; and half a dozen gadgets rejected by the Yanks as either too newfangled or unsuited to the American beaches—such as an armored flamethrower and a mine detector bolted to the nose of a tank—proved useful at several points during the battle.

In other respects, Gold, Juno, and Sword were similar to Utah and Omaha, if less benign than the former and less harrowing than the latter. Like on Omaha Beach, some amphibious Shermans foundered in the chop, and many LCT engine rooms flooded from leaks and the low freeboard, the distance between the waterline and the deck. Landing craft ferrying

This Centaur Mk IV tank made it to shore.
Photo taken on June 13.

Centaur tanks proved no more seaworthy than the DUKWs overloaded with American howitzers; scores capsized. OVER-LORD's eastern flank was considered especially vulnerable, so two battleships and a smaller monitor pounded the landscape with 15-inch guns from twenty thousand yards, buttressed by five cruisers and fifteen destroyers. Thousands of rockets launched from modified landing craft soared inland "like large packs of grouse going for the next parish with a strong wind under their tails," as one brigadier reported. This twenty-eight-mile stretch of coast was defended by ninety shore guns and eight German battalions whose ranks included many conscripted Poles, Czechs, and Ukrainians of doubtful loyalty to Germany. British naval and air bombardments later were found to have demolished one in ten enemy mortars, one in five machine guns, and one in three larger guns, in addition to those abandoned by their frightened crews. Still, British assault infantrymen were said to be disappointed, having "expected to find the Germans dead and not just disorganized."

GOLD

CLOSEST TO OMAHA lay Gold, barricaded with 2,500 obstacles along its 3.5-mile length. Engineers managed to clear only two boat lanes on the rising tide, and strong fortifications at Le Hamel would hold out until reduced by bombs and grenades later in the day. Royal Marines storming the fishing village of Port-en-Bessin, on the Omaha boundary, suffered over two hundred casualties during the forty-eight hours needed to finally rout enemy diehards there. But by early afternoon on June 6, all four brigades of the 50th Division made shore, hurrying inland and threatening to pass around the German flank.

SWORD

ON THE EASTERN LIP of the Allied beachhead, the British 3rd Division hit Sword on a narrow front in hopes of quickly knifing through to Caen, nine miles inland. "Ramp down! All out!" the boat crews cried, echoed by sergeants barking, "Bash on! Bash on!" Enemy mortar and machine-gun fire bashed back, and Royal Engineers cleared no beach obstacles on the first tide. Tommies "with shoulders hunched like boxers ready for in-fighting" found themselves in the surf, as a *Daily Mail* reporter wrote, "treading on an invisible carpet of squirming men." A Commando sergeant reported that the crimson-tinted seawater "made it look as though men were drowning in their own blood," and a lieutenant in the King's Liverpool Regiment told his diary: "Beach a shambles. Bodies everywhere. . . . Phil killed." The northwest wind shoved the high-tide line to within thirty feet of the dunes, leaving the narrow beach utterly clogged and so disrupting landing schedules that a reserve

British troops land on Sword Beach at 8:30 A.M.

Twenty-one-year-old Piper Bill Millin plays the bagpipes for men of the 1st Special Service Brigade who will embark for the invasion.

brigade remained at sea until midafternoon. Even so, Piper Bill Millin, wearing a kilt and with a dagger strapped to his leg, waded through the shallows playing "Highland Laddie" despite cries of "Get down, you mad bastard, you're attracting attention to us!" Millin then marched off with his troops to search for British glidermen holding the Orne bridges.

JUNO

THE WIND-WHIPPED TIDE and a bullying current also plagued the Canadian 3rd Division on Juno, wedged between the two British beaches. Almost one-third of three hundred landing craft were lost or damaged, and only six of forty tanks

British and Canadian troops land on Juno Beach.

made shore. Street fighting raged along the Courseulles harbor, and fortified houses behind the twelve-foot seawall at Bernières kept Canadian artillery and vehicles jammed on the beaches. Pigeons carrying Reuters news service dispatches from Juno flew south rather than across the Channel, provoking outraged cries of "Traitors! Damned traitors!"

Despite such setbacks and a thousand Canadian casualties—about half the number expected—by midmorning the Royal Winnipeg Rifles and Regina Rifles had pushed two miles inland. Once troops punched through the coastal defenses, few German units remained to block village crossroads. At two P.M., Piper Millin and the Commandos, led by their brigadier, Simon Fraser, Lord Lovat, tramped across the Bénouville bridge held by Major John Howard and his glider force; on this small piece of land the seaborne and airborne forces were now linked. Fifteen miles to the west, Allied fighter-bombers at noon pounced on a counterattacking regiment of twenty-five hundred Germans with twenty-two assault guns near Villiers-le-Sec. British troops from Gold Beach finished the rout at three P.M., killing the German commander and shattering the enemy column.

Reporters were told to expect a briefing by British officers at four P.M. in Caen. No such briefing took place: the 3rd Division spearhead, harassed by mines and heavy gunfire, stalled three miles north of the city. Troops from the Royal Warwickshire Regiment who were issued bicycles and told to "cycle like mad behind the Sherman tanks into Caen" found bikes "not at all the ideal accessory" for crawling under mortar fire. The city and the road linking the town to Bayeux remained in German hands, an inconvenience both vexing and consequential.

Yet the day seemed undimmed. Canadian troops had pressed six miles or more into France, and British soldiers reported reaching Bayeux's outskirts. Despite sniper fire nagging from a nearby wood, engineers by day's end began building a refueling airstrip at Crépon with a twelve-hundred-foot packed-earth runway. Prisoners trudged to cages on the beach, holding up trousers from which the buttons had been snipped to discourage flight. French women who emerged from cellars to kiss their liberators found themselves happily smudged with camouflage kettle soot and linseed oil. Inquiries by officers in their public-school French—*"Où sont les Boches?"* "Where are the German soldiers?"—often provoked wild pointing and an incomprehensible torrent of Norman dialect. But there was no misunderstanding the scratchy strains of "La Marseillaise," France's national anthem, played over and over by a young girl outside her cottage on an antique gramophone with a tin horn. *Allons enfants de la Patrie, / Le jour de gloire est arrivé!* Arise, children of the Fatherland / The day of glory has arrived!

German prisoners held in a barbed wire enclosure on Utah Beach.

ON THE OTHER SIDE OF THE LINE: FIELD MARSHAL ERWIN ROMMEL

General Field Marshal Erwin Rommel with General Field Marshal Gerd von Rundstedt at Rommel's headquarters in June 1944.

AS IF IN PURSUIT of the sinking sun, a black Horch convertible raced west across France from the German frontier, threading the Marne Valley from Reims, then swinging to the right bank of the Seine north of Paris. Since early May, Allied fighter-bombers had demolished all twenty-six bridges spanning the river from the French capital to the sea, converting the pretty, rural drive to Normandy into a circuitous annoyance. The sleek Horch, with its winged chrome ornament on the radiator grille and twin spare tires mounted behind the front fenders, provoked stares as the car sped through drowsy villages and farm communities. But it was the German officer in a leather coat in the front seat with a map spread across his knees who drew the eye: the familiar flat face, with a narrow, sloping forehead and the beginnings of jowls, belonged to Adolf Hitler's youngest but most celebrated field marshal. Even French peasants recognized him, and as the convertible raced past they called aloud to one another: *"C'est Rommel!"*

Yes, Rommel. He had driven home to Herrlingen in southwest Germany the previous day with a pair of gray suede shoes from Paris as a surprise fiftieth-birthday present for his wife, Lucie-Maria. He had meant to confer afterward with Führer Hitler in his mountain retreat at Berchtesgaden and to complain about shortages of men and matériel for the Atlantic Wall, but he had instead been summoned back to France by grave reports of Allied landings in Normandy on Tuesday morning. *"Tempo!"* he urged the driver. *"Tempo!"* Turning to an aide in the rear seat, he added, "If I was commander of the Allied forces right now, I could finish off the war in fourteen days."

At 9:30 P.M., with little left of the long summer day, sentries in camouflage capes waved the Horch into the red-roofed river village of La Roche–Guyon, forty miles west of Paris. The car turned right through a spiked wrought-iron gate to stop with a screech in a stone courtyard. The Château de la Roche–Guyon had presided above this great loop of the Seine since the twelfth century and had served since early March as Rommel's Army Group B headquarters. Clutching his silver-capped staff, the field marshal climbed a flight of steps to the main door, determined to salvage what he could from the day's catastrophe.

Clacking typewriters and snatches of music by Wilhelm Richard Wagner playing on a phonograph could be heard as Rommel ascended the grand staircase and hurried through the billiards room to the salon that now served as his office. He stood, hands clasped behind his back, listening as staff officers sought to make sense of the sixth of June. "He's very calm and collected," an artillery officer wrote. "Grim-faced, as is to be expected."

There was much to be grim about. Thanks to Allied jamming and downed phone lines, little was known with certainty. Somehow thousands of ships had crossed the English Channel undetected. No German reconnaissance planes had flown for the first five days of June, and naval patrols on June 5 were scrubbed because of the nasty weather. A decoded radio message—intercepted about the time the 101st Airborne launched from England—suggested a possible invasion within forty-eight hours. But an advisory on Monday evening from OB West, the German headquarters for western Europe, declared,

German soldiers operating an Enigma machine, used to encipher and decipher messages.

"There are no signs yet of an imminent invasion." Besides Rommel, two of the top four German commanders in the west had been away from their posts on Tuesday morning, and several senior field officers in Normandy had driven to Rennes, in Brittany, for a map exercise. The Fifteenth Army, near the Pas de Calais, was placed on full alert before midnight, but the other major component of Rommel's Army Group B, the Seventh Army occupying Normandy, sounded no general alarm until 1:30 A.M. despite reports of paratroopers near Caen and in the Cotentin Peninsula. Even then, OB West insisted at 2:40 A.M.: "It is not a major action."

Not until that fantastic fleet materialized from the mist had the truth struck home. In subsequent hours the German navy remained inactive; so too the air force. Luftwaffe pilots were supposed to fly up to five daily missions each to disrupt any invasion, but German aircraft losses in the past five months exceeded 13,000 planes, more than half from accidents and other noncombat causes such as fuel depletion and crashes during night flights. Air Fleet Three, responsible for western France, had just 319 serviceable planes facing nearly 13,000 Allied aircraft; on D-Day, they would fly one mission for every thirty-seven flown by their adversaries. Of the mere dozen German fighter-bombers that reached the invasion zone, ten dropped their bombs prematurely. German soldiers now bitterly joked that American planes were gray, British planes black, and Luftwaffe planes invisible.

Still, Seventh Army asserted through much of the day that at least part of the Allied landing had been halted at the water's edge. "The enemy, penetrating our positions, was thrown back into the sea," the 352nd Infantry Division reported at 1:35 P.M. That soap-bubble delusion soon popped: at six P.M. the division acknowledged "unfavorable developments," including Allied troops infiltrating inland and nosing toward Bayeux.

Rommel's grim face grew grimmer. Here in Normandy, at the beginning of the war, he had first made his name as "the fighting animal," in one biographer's phrase, driving his 7th Panzer Division more than two hundred miles in four days to trap the French garrison at Cherbourg in June 1940. Soon after, in Africa, the fighting animal became known as the Desert Fox, although even he could not forestall the Allied triumph in Tunisia. After that, he told a comrade, he hoped "to re-win great fame in the West."

Hitler's decision in November 1943 to reinforce the

Atlantic Wall against "an Anglo-Saxon landing" offered Rommel that chance. As commander of half a million men in Army Group B, with responsibility for the coast from Holland to Saint-Nazaire, France, where the Loire River meets the sea, the field marshal had flung himself into building the "Rommel Belt." In all, 20,000 coastal fortifications had been constructed, 500,000 obstacles placed along the shore, and 6.5 million mines planted in what he called "the zone of death." To Lucie-Maria he wrote on May 19, "The enemy will have a rough time of it when he attacks, and ultimately achieve no success." Hitler agreed, declaring, "Once defeated, the enemy will never try to invade again."

If confident enough to travel home for his wife's birthday,

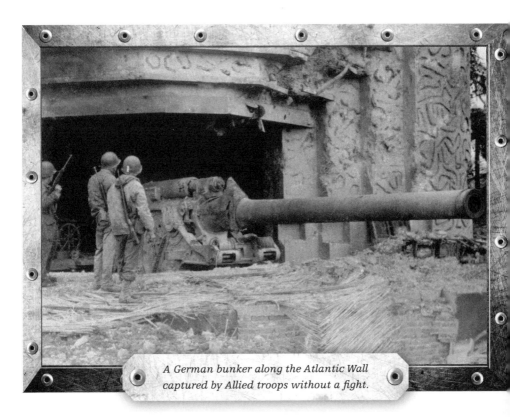

A German bunker along the Atlantic Wall captured by Allied troops without a fight.

Rommel harbored few illusions. Two years of campaigning in Africa gave him great faith in land mines, but he wanted 200 million of them, not 6.5 million. Some of his divisions were composed of older troops, as well as many non-Germans—paybooks had been issued in eight different languages just for former Soviet citizens now serving the Wehrmacht. Army Group B relied on 67,000 horses for transport; across the entire front, fewer than 15,000 trucks could be found. A corps commander in Normandy complained, "Emplacements without guns, ammunition depots without ammunition, minefields without mines, and a large number of men in uniform with hardly a soldier among them."

Worse yet was the Anglo-American advantage in airpower and seapower. Seventy-one thousand tons of Allied bombs had already destroyed the German transportation system in the west. Train traffic in France had declined 60 percent since March. Allied fighter sweeps proved so murderous that German daytime rail movement in France was banned after May 26. Beyond the 45,000 armed railwaymen already transferred from Germany to stop saboteurs, almost 30,000 workers were brought in from the Atlantic Wall for rail repair duties. Some field commanders, Rommel grumbled, "do not seem to have recognized the graveness of the hour." Six weeks earlier he had warned subordinates:

The enemy will most likely try to land at night and by fog, after a tremendous shelling by artillery and bombers. They will employ hundreds of boats and ships unloading amphibious vehicles and waterproof

submersible tanks. We must stop him in the water, not only delay him. . . . The enemy must be annihilated before he reaches our main battlefield.

In this command lay what one German general called "a cock-fight controversy." For months the high command had bickered about how best to thwart an Allied invasion. Rommel argued that "the main battle line must be the beach," with armored reserves poised near the coast. "If we can't throw the enemy into the sea within twenty-four hours," he told officers in Normandy, "then that will be the beginning of the end." In March he had proposed that all armored, mechanized, and artillery units in the west be bundled under his command,

and that he assume some control over the First and Nineteenth Armies in southern France.

This impertinence found little favor in Berlin or Paris. The OB West commander, Field Marshal Gerd von Rundstedt, who called his brash subordinate "an unlicked cub" and "the Marshal Laddie," argued that to disperse counterattack forces along seventeen hundred miles of exposed Atlantic and Mediterranean coastline would be foolhardy. Better to concentrate a central mobile reserve near Paris, able to strike as a clenched fist whenever and wherever the invaders committed themselves.

Hitler dithered, then ordered a compromise that pleased no one. Frontline forces on the coast were to fight "to the last man"—that phrase so easily uttered by those far from the trenches—and Army Group B would command three armored divisions among the ten on the Western Front. Three others went to southern France. The remaining four, controlled by Berlin, were clustered near Paris in a strategic ensemble called Panzer Group West. Neither Rundstedt nor Rommel could issue orders to air or naval forces, who were vaguely advised to cooperate with ground commanders. Just a few days earlier, Hitler had shifted troops from OB West to Italy and the Eastern Front. Perhaps predictably, when frantic pleas to release the armored reserves had arrived in Berlin and Berchtesgaden this morning, more than eight hours passed before the panzers were ordered to begin the long, tortuous journey toward Normandy. Rommel denounced the delay as "madness," adding, "Of course now they will arrive too late."

Dusk sifted over the Seine Valley. The day's last light faded from the chalk cliffs above the château, where antiaircraft

Adolf Hitler (right) congratulates Erwin Rommel on February 6, 1940, when he gave Rommel command of Germany's elite armored troops.

gunners strained for the drone of approaching bombers. Telephones jangled in the salon war room, and orderlies crisscrossed the floor with the latest scraps of news.

The struggle in Normandy would depend in large measure on the only armored unit within quick striking distance of the invasion beaches, the 21st Panzer Division. A stalwart from Africa, the division had been obliterated in Tunisia, then rebuilt with sixteen thousand men—some still wearing remnants of tropical uniforms—and 127 tanks. Even while racing back to France this afternoon, Rommel had stopped midway to confirm by phone that the unit was hurrying into action. Now the harsh truth became clear: orders, counterorders, and disorder had plagued the division almost as much as marauding Allied planes and scorching field-gun fire. Not least among the 21st's troubles was the temporary absence of Rommel, their commanding general. The division's antiaircraft battalion had been pulverized by Allied naval gunfire north of Caen, and the tank regiment gutted both from the air and by British gunners. This evening a panzer grenadier regiment moving toward Sword Beach in the two-mile gap between Canadian and British troops had nearly reached the strand. Then, just before nine P.M., almost 250 more British gliders escorted by fighters swept into the Orne Valley, doubling British airborne combat power in France and threatening to pin the grenadiers against the sea.

At 10:40 P.M., General Friedrich Dollmann, who had commanded Seventh Army since 1939, phoned La Roche–Guyon with dire news. The "strong attack by the 21st Panzer Division has been smothered by new airborne landings," Dollmann reported. The counterattack had failed. Nearly two-thirds of the 21st Panzer's tanks were lost. Swarming enemy aircraft impeded movement, even at night. Grenadiers skulked back from the coast to defensive positions in the hills around Caen with only two dozen 88mm guns.

Rommel hung up the phone. Hands again clasped behind his back, he studied the wall map. The critical crossroads city of Caen remained in German hands, and nowhere did the Anglo-American penetration appear deeper than a few kilometers. The 12th SS Panzer and the Panzer Lehr Divisions were finally moving toward Normandy despite fighter-bombers flocking to the telltale dust clouds like raptors to prey. "We cannot hold everything," Rommel would tell his chief of staff. The critical first twenty-four hours were nearly over, yet perhaps the coastal battle could still be saved. He turned to an aide and said, as if reminding himself, "I've nearly always succeeded up to now." He was, as ever, the führer's marshal.

AS THE FULL MOON RISES

A MONSTROUS FULL MOON rose over the beachhead, where 156,000 Allied soldiers burrowed in as best they could to snatch an hour of sleep. Rommel was right: the invaders' grip on France was tenuous, ranging from six miles beyond Gold and Juno to barely two thousand yards beyond Omaha. A crude sod airstrip had opened alongside Utah Beach at 9:15 P.M., the first of 241 airstrips the Americans would build across western Europe in the next eleven months. Yet only 100 tons of supplies made shore by midnight, rather than the 2,400 tons planned. Paratroopers, particularly among the nineteen airborne battalions on the American western flank, fought as scattered gangs in a score or more of muddled, desperate gunfights. Every man who survived the day now knew in his bones, as one paratrooper wrote, that "we were there for one purpose, to kill each other."

If the 21st Panzer had failed to fulfill Rommel's imperative

*An aerial view of the bombing
of Caen at 1:30 P.M., June 6.*

to beat the enemy into the sea within twenty-four hours, the division *had* blocked the capture of Caen, gateway to the rolling terrain leading toward Paris. "I must have Caen," the British Second Army commander, Lieutenant General Miles Dempsey, had declared at St. Paul's School three weeks earlier. But he would not have it today, or any day soon, in part because his landing force was unprepared to fight enemy armored forces and vehicles so soon. Even so, a British captain wrote, "We were not unpleased with ourselves."

All told, three thousand Normans would be killed on June

6 and 7 by bombs, naval shells, and bullets; they joined fifteen thousand French civilians already dead from months of bombardment before the invasion. Some injured citizens were reduced to disinfecting their wounds with Calvados, the local brandy fermented from apples. "Liberation," wrote the journalist Alan Moorehead, "usually meant excessive hardship for the first few months."

As for the liberators, the eight assault divisions now ashore had suffered 12,000 killed, wounded, and missing, with thousands more unaccounted for, most of whom had simply gone off course in the chaos. Allied aircraft losses in the invasion totaled 127. The 8,230 U.S. casualties on D-Day included the first of almost 400,000 men who would be wounded in the European theater, the first of 7,000 amputations, the first of 89,000 fractures. Many were felled by 9.6-gram bullets moving at 2,000 to 4,000 feet per second, or by shell fragments traveling even faster. Aboard U.S.S. *Samuel Chase*, mess boys who that morning had served breakfast in white jackets were now as blood-smeared as slaughterhouse workers from sewing corpses into burial sacks. A British doctor who spent Tuesday evening on Sword Beach reported that, for most of the wounded, "nothing was being done for them as there was no plasma or blood, and they lay there being bombed and machine-gunned all night long." On Utah, handkerchiefs draped the faces of the dead.

Omaha was the worst, of course. Stretcher bearers with blistered hands carried broken boys down the bluff to Easy Red—now dubbed Dark Red—only to find that a medical

An amphibious DUKW that brought soldiers to the beaches is now used to transport wounded soldiers to medical ships.

battalion had come ashore with typewriters and office files but no surgical equipment or morphine. Blankets were stripped from the dead or salvaged from the shoreline between outbursts of German artillery. Fearful of mines and rough surf, most landing craft refused to pick up casualties from the beach after dark. A single ambulance with cat's-eye headlights crept along the dunes, delivering the wounded to collection-point trenches, where medics plucked scraps of GI boot leather from mine wounds. They hushed sufferers who asked only for a bullet in the brain. A soldier returning to Omaha for ammunition found many comrades "out of their heads. There were men crying, men moaning, and there were men screaming."

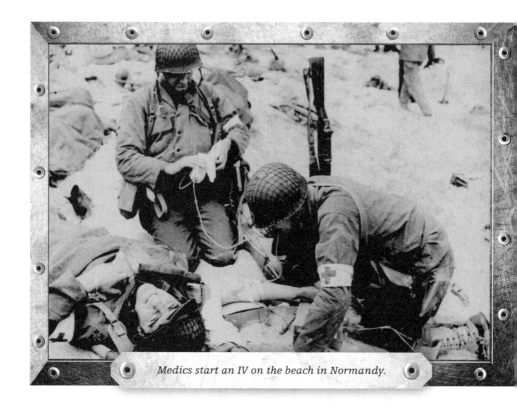

Medics start an IV on the beach in Normandy.

Others were beyond screams. Dead men lay in rows like "swollen grayish sacks," in one reporter's image. "I walked along slowly, counting bodies," wrote the correspondent Gordon Gaskill, who prowled the beach on Tuesday evening. "Within 400 paces I counted 221 of them." More than double that number—487—would be gathered on Omaha, toes sticking up in a line as if at parade drill. "One came up on them rather too suddenly and wanted to stare hard," a navy lieutenant wrote, "but there was that feeling that staring was rude."

Graves Registration teams tied Emergency Medical Tag #52B to each corpse for identification, then shrouded them in mattress covers fastened with safety pins. Two inland sites had been chosen for cemeteries but both remained under fire, so temporary graves were scooped out below the cliff. Shovel details fortified with brandy buried their comrades in haste.

So ended the day, unparalleled and soon legendary, and perhaps indeed, as in the judgment of a Royal Air Force history, "the most momentous in the history of war since Alexander set out from Macedon." In southern England, the first German prisoners arrived on an LST. Martha Gellhorn studied the "small shabby men in field gray . . . trying to see in those faces what had happened in the world." A badly wounded American lieutenant, evacuated on a surgical stretcher next to a German shot in the chest and legs, murmured, "I'd kill him if I could move."

The first transport ship carrying 1,096 German prisoners arrives in England.

Such bloodthirsty purpose would be needed in the weeks and months ahead. For the moment, the Allies savored their triumph. "We will never again have to land under fire," a navy officer wrote his wife on June 7. "This is the end of Germany and Japan." If too optimistic—assault landings were still to come in southern France and on various Pacific islands—the core sentiment held. For four years Hitler had fortified this coast, most recently entrusting the task to his most charismatic general, yet Allied assault troops had needed less than three hours to crack the Atlantic Wall and burst into Fortress Europe. Though far from over, the battle was won.

"We have come to the hour for which we were born," a *New York Times* editorial declared on Wednesday morning. "We go forth to meet the supreme test of our arms and of our souls." Yet even as the dead still lay on the Norman sand, silvered by the rising moon, toes pointing toward the stars, the living would carry them along. "I shall never forget that beach," Corporal William Preston, who had come ashore at dawn in an amphibious tank, wrote to his family in New York. Nor would he forget one dead soldier in particular who caught his eye. "I wonder about him," Preston added. "What were his plans never to be fulfilled, what fate brought him to that spot at that moment? Who was waiting for him at home?" Many of those who went forth on that day to test their arms and their souls were lost, and many more would die each day until the victory was won.

COMPLETE NEWS—MAGAZINE SECTION—COMIC FEATURES

New York Post

FOUNDED 1801 VOLUME 143, NO. 169 COPYRIGHT, 1944, NEW YORK POST.

5¢

 BLUE 7 FINAL LAST SPORTS PAGE

TWO SECTIONS   NEW YORK, TUESDAY, JUNE 6, 1944   40 PAGES

INVASION

SMASHING AHEAD!

Nazis Say We're 10 Miles In; Sky Troops Far Beyond Lines

Combatants from the Free French Army march down the Champs-Élysées on August 6, 1944, when Paris was liberated.

A Russian soldier raises the Soviet flag over the Reichstag, the historic parliament building in Berlin.

EPILOGUE:
THE DAYS THAT FOLLOWED

IN THE NEXT 338 days, Allied troops in western Europe advanced more than seven hundred miles, liberated oppressed peoples by the tens of millions, seized a hundred thousand square miles of Germany and Austria, captured more than four million prisoners, and killed or badly wounded an estimated one million enemy soldiers.

On that last day, May 7, 1945, the *Daily Mail* in London reported that a dozen elderly men stood for hours "with ropes in their hands and hope in their hearts, waiting

Prime Minister Winston Churchill is mobbed on V-E Day.

to send the bells of St. Paul's Church clanging . . . in triumph." In vain they stood: no bell pealed. They would wait another day until Moscow attained a written surrender from the German troops on the Eastern Front.

But there had been an official signing ceremony in France. At a redbrick schoolhouse that served as the SHAEF headquarters in Reims, German general Alfred Jodl signed a document of unconditional surrender. Word of the Reims ceremony had leaked—even to Germany. A German radio broadcast from Flensburg on Monday announced the end, and an Associated Press reporter who had witnessed the signing disobeyed Eisenhower's news embargo by sending word to New York, where ticker tape soon fluttered. "It will seem that it is only the governments who do not know," British prime minister Winston Churchill cabled Russian leader Joseph Stalin at 4:30 P.M. Monday.

But Stalin remained adamant that another document be signed in Soviet-controlled Berlin. Churchill and U.S. president Harry Truman reluctantly agreed to withhold confirmation of the surrender. V-E Day— victory in Europe—would

General Field Marshal Wilhelm Keitel signs the unconditional surrender of Germany in the Soviet Army headquarters in Berlin, Germany.

not become official until Tuesday, May 8. Eisenhower dispatched a SHAEF delegation to meet the Soviets at a former German military engineering school in Karlshorst, ten miles southeast of central Berlin. Here the Germans would surrender, again, after nine hours of noisy haggling.

Notwithstanding a BBC announcement at six P.M. on Monday that V-E Day must wait until the next day, a boisterous, expectant throng jammed London's Piccadilly and Trafalgar Squares. "V-E Day may be tomorrow," the *Daily Mail* declared, "but the war is over tonight." Bonfires glazed the clouds with an orange tint. Yet as word of the postponement spread, the festive spirit fizzled. "Move along," a policeman ordered. "It's all off."

In Paris, a celebration that began Monday night would run riot until midday Thursday. Jeeps packed with GIs and French women cruised the streets as crowds shouted, "*Salut! Vive les États-Unis!*" Snaking throngs danced down the Champs-Élysées as sirens sounded a final all-clear and church bells rang across the city. So many filled the Place de la Concorde that American MPs struggled to open a corridor into the U.S. embassy; thousands joined the Yanks in singing, or at least humming, "The Battle Hymn of the Republic." For the first time since the war began,

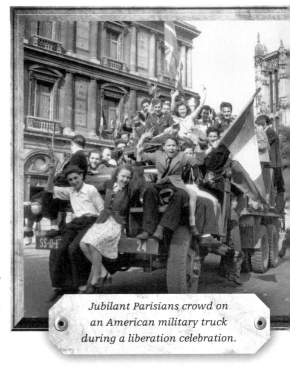

Jubilant Parisians crowd on an American military truck during a liberation celebration.

lights illuminated the Arc de Triomphe, the Opéra, and other grand landmarks.

The rest of the world soon caught the celebratory spirit. A crowd estimated at five thousand gathered in front of the U.S. embassy near Red Square in Moscow to cheer the American ally; Yanks spotted in the street were playfully tossed into the air. In New York City, half a million celebrants filled Times Square, and enormous headlines splashed across page one of the *New York Times* proclaimed, THE WAR IN EUROPE IS ENDED! SURRENDER IS UNCONDITIONAL; V-E WILL BE PROCLAIMED TODAY. In Washington, D.C., lights bathed the Capitol dome for the first time since the U.S. declared war on December 8, 1941. Harry Truman, who became president on Roosevelt's sudden death

V-E Day celebration in New York City.

on April 12, 1945, told the nation, "This is a solemn but glorious hour. We must work to finish the war. Our victory is only half won. The West is free, but the East is still in bondage to the treacherous Japanese."

May 8 dawned in London with thunder so violent that many woke fearing a return of German bombers. By midmorning the storm had rolled off, the sun broke through, and those St. Paul's bell-ringers leaned into their work. Crowds outside Buckingham Palace chanted, "We want the king!" and the king they got, along with the queen and two princesses, who appeared waving from a balcony six times during the day.

In London, Princess Elizabeth, Queen Elizabeth the Queen Mother, Winston Churchill, King George VI, and Princess Margaret appear on the balcony of Buckingham Palace.

By the time Japan signed formal surrender documents on September 2, 1945, the Second World War had lasted six years and a day, involving more than sixty nations, plus other colonial and imperial territories. Sixty million had died in those six years, including nearly 10 million in Germany and Japan, and more than twice that number in the Soviet Union—roughly 26 million, one-third of them soldiers. To describe this "great and terrible epoch," as George Marshall—Truman's army chief of staff and architect of the United States's new army—called it, new words would be required, like "genocide"; and old words would assume new usages, like "Holocaust."

For the Allies, some solace could be derived from complete victory over a foe of unprecedented evil. The solidarity and cooperation of the Allied countries had ensured victory: the better alliance had won. In contrast to the Axis autocracy,

General MacArthur reads the terms of surrender to Japanese officials on board the U.S.S. Missouri on September 2, 1945.

Allied leadership included checks and balances to temper arbitrary willfulness and personal misjudgment. The battlefield had offered a proving ground upon which demonstrated competence and clearheadedness could flourish; as usual, modern war also rewarded ingenuity, collaboration, organizational skill, and, of course, luck.

Resolution and courage both proved equal to the cause, as did more material contributions. The Americans had provided more than two-thirds of the Allies' 91 divisions, and half of the 28,000 combat aircraft. The entire war had cost U.S. taxpayers $296 billion—roughly $4 trillion in 2012 dollars. The armed forces had grown 3,500 percent while building 3,000 overseas bases and depots, and shipping 4.5 tons of matériel abroad for each soldier deployed, plus another ton each month to sustain him.

What Churchill called the American "prodigy of organization" had delivered 18 million tons of war stuff to Europe, equivalent to the cargo in 181,000 railcars: the supplies ranged from 800,000 military vehicles to footwear in sizes from 2A to 22EEE. U.S. munitions plants had turned out 40 billion rounds of small arms ammunition and 56 million grenades. From D-Day to V-E Day, GIs fired 500 million machine-gun bullets and 23 million artillery rounds. By 1945, the United States

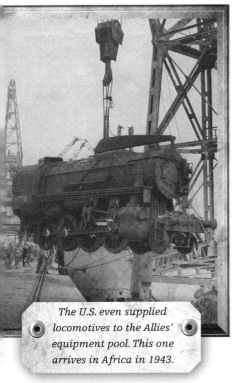

The U.S. even supplied locomotives to the Allies' equipment pool. This one arrives in Africa in 1943.

had built two-thirds of all ships afloat and was making half of all manufactured goods in the world, including nearly half of all armaments. The enemy was crushed by logistical brilliance, firepower, mobility, mechanical aptitude, and an economic force that produced much, much more of nearly everything than Germany could—bombers, bombs, fighters, transport planes, mortars, machine guns, trucks.

The war was a potent catalyst for social change across the U.S. New technologies—jets, computers, ballistic missiles, penicillin—soon spurred vibrant new industries, which in turn encouraged the migration of black workers from south to north, and of all peoples to the emerging west. The GI Bill put millions of soldiers into college classrooms, leading to unprecedented social mobility. Nineteen million American women on the home front had entered the workplace by war's end; although they quickly reverted to traditional roles—the percentage working in 1947 was hardly higher than it had been in 1940—that genie would not remain back in the bottle forever.

In battered Europe, enormous tasks remained. Those who had outlived the war had to "learn how to reassemble our broken world," as American reporter Ernie Pyle put it. The last debris of the Third Reich had to be swept up, including 400,000 German troops adrift in

American women worked in airplane factories during the war.

Norway. Not least among the jobs at hand was the disposal of 211,000 tons of German poisonous gas munitions found in the U.S. and British zones alone, including 90,000 tons of mustard bombs and 3.7 million gas artillery shells—a reminder of how much worse the war could have been.

"On the continent of Europe we have yet to make sure that . . . the words 'freedom,' 'democracy,' and 'liberation' are not distorted from their true meaning as we have understood them," Churchill told his countrymen in mid-May. "Forward, unflinching, unswerving, indomitable, till the whole task is done and the whole world safe and clean." Part of that cleansing required the investigation and prosecution of those guilty for murdering six million Jews, half a million Gypsies, and others—many others. Three thousand tons of documents relating to the concentration camps would be captured and studied. In Room 600 of the courthouse in Nuremberg, Germany, the most celebrated of all war-crimes tribunals would hear testimony from 360 witnesses and review 200,000 affidavits. Of two dozen major Nazi defendants, ten would be hanged in October 1946, from gallows built in a jail gymnasium.

Former Nazi leaders on trial at Nuremberg in 1946.

Eisenhower's avowed "number one plan" after the war was "to sit on the bank of a quiet stream and fish." That would not happen; the victorious commander was destined for grander things. Among the many accolades he received, no laurel meant more to Eisenhower than George Marshall's tribute:

You have completed your mission with the greatest victory in the history of warfare. . . . You have made history, great history for the good of all mankind, and you have stood for all we hope for and admire in an officer of the United States Army.

Ahead lay fifteen more years of service, as army chief of staff, president of Columbia University, commander of the new NATO military alliance, and president of his country. But first Eisenhower would return to London, where three years earlier he had arrived as a new and quite anonymous major general responsible for planning the liberation of Europe. Now a mob instantly gathered when he tried to take a quiet stroll through Hyde Park—"Ike! Good old Ike!" they cried.

On Tuesday, June 12, in an open carriage pulled by a pair of high-stepping horses, he rode to the Guildhall, London's

Dwight D. Eisenhower is sworn in as president of the United States on January 20, 1953.

eight-hundred-year-old city hall, still scarred from German bombs. Here he would receive a sword of honor and Britain's formal thanks. A bailiff bellowed from the door, "The supreme commander of the Allied Expeditionary Force!" Eisenhower climbed to the dais to be welcomed with applause by the great men of England, Churchill foremost among them. For twenty minutes, pale and a bit nervous, he spoke without notes of their common cause, their shared sacrifice, and their joint victory. One line from Eisenhower's address would be engraved over his tomb in Kansas a quarter-century later: "Humility must always be the portion of any man who receives acclaim earned in the blood of his followers and the sacrifices of his friends."

Blood there had surely been, and sacrifices beyond comprehension. Battle casualties among armies of the Western Allies since D-Day exceeded three-quarters of a million, of whom at least 165,000 were dead. Added to that were 10,000 naval losses, half of them dead, and 62,000 air casualties—half of them dead, too, in the 12,000 Allied planes lost over Europe.

American soldiers bore the brunt for the Western armies in the climactic final year: the 587,000 U.S. casualties in western Europe included 135,576 dead, almost half of the number of existing U.S. troops worldwide. Of 361,000 wounded GIs, the quick and the lucky escaped with superficial scars, like the veteran who years later wrote that "my left index finger still carries the mark where a tiny shell fragment entered it once, back there one raving afternoon." Others were less fortunate, among them the 1,700 left blind, and the 11,000 with at least partial paralysis of one or more limbs. The army also tallied 18,000 amputations, most of which occurred after June

1944. The numbers during the six years at war from the Allied countries were staggering: in the Soviet Union, almost nine million soldiers and eighteen million civilians dead; in the U.K. 383,000 soldiers and 70,000 civilians; in Canada 45,400 soldiers dead.

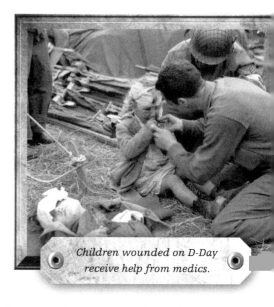

Children wounded on D-Day receive help from medics.

On June 6, 1944, just prior to the invasion, General Dwight Eisenhower sent this message to the men and women under his command:

Soldiers, Sailors and Airmen of the Allied Expeditionary Force! You are about to embark upon a great crusade, toward which we have striven these many months. The eyes of the world are upon you. The hopes and prayers of liberty loving people everywhere march with you. In company with our brave Allies and brothers in arms on other fronts, you will bring about the destruction of the German war machine, the elimination of Nazi tyranny over the oppressed peoples of Europe, and security for ourselves in a free world. . . .

I have full confidence in your courage, devotion to duty and skill in battle. We will accept nothing less than full victory!

Good Luck! And let us all beseech the blessings of Almighty God upon this great and noble undertaking.

On May 8, 1945, 338 days later, he was able to say:

The crusade on which we embarked in the early summer of 1944 has reached its glorious conclusion. It is my especial privilege, in the name of all nations represented in this theatre of war, to commend each of you for the valiant performance of duty. . . .

General Eisenhower salutes troops and civilians in liberated Paris, August 29, 1945.

Full victory in Europe has been attained. Working and fighting together in single and indestructible partnership you have achieved a perfection in the unification of air, ground and naval power that will stand as a model in our time.

The route you have traveled through hundreds of miles is marked by the graves of former comrades. From them have been exacted the ultimate sacrifice. The blood of many nations—American, British, Canadian, French, Polish and others—has helped to gain the victory. Each of the fallen died as a member of a team to which you belong, bound together by a common love of liberty and a refusal to submit to enslavement. No monument of stone, no memorial of whatever magnitude could so well express our respect and veneration for their sacrifice as would the perpetuation of the spirit of comradeship in which they died.

As we celebrate victory in Europe let us remind ourselves that our common problems of the immediate and distant future can be best solved in the same conceptions of cooperation and devotion to the cause of human freedom as have made this Expeditionary Force such a mighty engine of righteous destruction. Let us have no part in the profitless quarrels in which other men will inevitably engage as to what country and what service won the European war.

Every man and every woman of every nation here represented has served according to his or her ability and efforts and each has contributed to the outcome. This we shall remember and in doing so we shall be revering each honored grave and be sending comfort to the loved ones of comrades who could not live to see this day.

Three Canadians from the Army Medical Corps place flowers on temporary graves in Normandy, June 1944.

THE UNITED STATES DECLARATION OF WAR ON GERMANY

ON DECEMBER 7, 1941, Japanese bombers attacked the U.S. Navy base at Pearl Harbor, Hawaii. President Roosevelt asked Congress for a declaration of war on Japan. That was issued on December 8. Japan then declared war on the U.S., as did Germany. On December 11, 1941, the Congress declared war on Germany.

This text was signed by President Roosevelt at 3:05 P.M.

Seventy-seventh Congress of the United States of America;

At the First Session

Begun and held at the City of Washington on Friday, the third
day of January, one thousand nine hundred and forty-one

JOINT RESOLUTION

Declaring that a state of war exists between the Government of
Germany and the Government and the people of the United States
and making provision to prosecute the same.

Whereas the Government of Germany has formally declared war
against the Government and the people of the United States of
America: Therefore be it

*Resolved by the Senate and House of Representatives of the United
States of America in Congress assembled*, That the state of war
between the United States and the Government of Germany which
has thus been thrust upon the United States is hereby formally
declared; and the President is hereby authorized and directed to
employ the entire naval and military forces of the United States
and the resources of the Government to carry on war against the
Government of Germany; and, to bring the conflict to a successful
termination, all of the resources of the country are hereby pledged
by the Congress of the United States.

Speaker of the House of Representatives.

H A Wallace

*Vice President of the United States and
President of the Senate.*

Approved
December 11 1941   305 p.m. E.S.T.

Franklin D Roosevelt

THE FIVE GREATEST TANKS OF THE WAR

AMERICAN M4 SHERMAN

American tanks are named for Civil War generals. The M4 Sherman could fire while on the move because it had a 75mm gun in a turret that swept right and left. One drawback was that its fuel tank easily caught fire.

GERMAN PANTHER

Regarded as one of the best tank designs of the war (although many of the elements were copied from the Soviet T-34), it suffered from advanced technology engineering that was difficult to repair in the field.

Sherman tank

GERMAN PzKFW MK. IV PANZER

The most used German tank of the war, it was designed to support infantry but eventually began engaging in battle.

GERMAN TIGER I/II

With heavy armor and strong guns, this tank was the most fearsome in the war, effective against both air and ground targets. It saw action on all German battlefronts.

SOVIET T-34

The most produced tank of the war, this effective and efficient machine is credited with winning the war on the Eastern Front.

THE LARGEST BATTLESHIPS OF THE WAR

U.S.S. Iowa

BECAUSE SUBMARINE and bomber attacks were such threats to this class of ship—and the potential losses so huge—battleships spent much of the war close to shore, helping with coastal bombardment.

I.N.S. *YAMATO*, Japan	72,809 tons, 862 feet
I.N.S. *MUSASHI*, Japan	72,809 tons, 862 feet
U.S.S. *IOWA*, United States (BB-61)	55,710 tons, 887 feet
U.S.S. *NEW JERSEY*, United States (BB-62)	55,710 tons, 887 feet
U.S.S. *MISSOURI*, United States (BB-63)	55,710 tons, 887 feet
U.S.S. *WISCONSIN*, United States (BB-64)	55,710 tons, 887 feet
S.M.S. *BISMARCK*, Germany	50,153 tons, 823 feet
S.M.S. *TIRPITZ*, Germany	50,153 tons, 823 feet
RICHELIEU*, France	47,500 tons, 812 feet
***JEAN BART*,** France	47,500 tons, 812 feet
H.M.S. *HOOD*, Great Britain	46,200 tons, 860 feet

THE MOST EFFECTIVE BOMBERS OF THE WAR

R.A.F. day raiders over Berlin's official quarter.

BACK THEM UP

AICHI D3A (Japan)

This plane sank more Allied ships than any Axis plane. It was a dive bomber also used in kamikaze, or suicide, attacks.

AVRO LANCASTER (Britain)

This night bomber flew more than 150,000 missions over Germany. Fully loaded, it could carry ten tons of bombs and also had turrets and machine guns to defend itself.

B-17 FLYING FORTRESS (United States)

Boeing developed this long-range heavy bomber in 1935. It carried more than five tons of bombs and was designed to protect itself, rather than rely on covering support from other planes. A crew of ten manned thirteen machine guns aimed at every angle.

B-24 LIBERATOR (United States)

The U.S. produced 18,400 of these planes for the war effort. They flew over Germany and were also used in antisubmarine patrols above the Atlantic Ocean.

B-29 SUPERFORTRESS (United States)

This plane had extremely advanced electronics, including remote-controlled machine gun turrets. It carried bombs inside the plane body and under each wing. The atomic bombs dropped on the Japanese cities of Hiroshima and Nagasaki were delivered by this type of plane.

DE HAVILLAND MOSQUITO (Britain)

Carrying one 1.8-ton bomb, this plane was highly accurate and fast. It was often sent out at night. Made of wood, the Mosquito was almost undetectable by radar.

HEINKEL III (Germany)

This plane was developed before World War II, when Germany was still forbidden to make armaments as a result of their loss in World War I. Perhaps the most recognizable of the German bombers, it was used exclusively in Europe, serving as a torpedo bomber and occasionally as a glider tug.

JUNKERS 87 STUKA (Germany)

Used in German surprise attacks, called blitzkriegs, this plane had a loud siren in its nose that became the signal for horrifying German bombing raids.

JUNKERS JU-88 (Germany)

Modified throughout the war, this plane was used as a fighter bomber, a night fighter, or a dive bomber.

MITSUBISHI G4M3 (Japan)

The most recognizable of Japanese planes, this was called the "Flying Cigar." It flew at high speeds and could go long distances before refueling.

WEAPONS CARRIED BY U.S., U.K., CANADIAN, AND GERMAN GROUND TROOPS

PISTOLS

- Webley Revolver – Britain
- Colt M1911 – United States
- Walther P38 and Luger P08 – Germany

BOLT–ACTION RIFLES

- Lee-Enfield SMLE – Britain
- M1903 Springfield – United States

SEMIAUTOMATIC RIFLES

- M1 Carbine – United States

SUBMACHINE GUNS

- Sten Gun – Britain
- M3 – United States
- Thompson M1928A1 – United States
- MP 40 – Germany

ASSAULT RIFLES

- M50 – United States
- FG 42 – Germany
- StG 44 – Germany

LIGHT MACHINE GUNS

- Bren Gun – Britain
- M1919 Browning – United States
- MG 42 – Germany

HAND GRENADES

- N°36 Mills – Britain
- M2 – United States
- Model 24 Stielhandgranate – Germany

LIGHT MORTARS

- SBML 2-inch mortar – Britain
- M2 mortar – United States

ANTITANK WEAPONS

- PIAT – Britain
- M1/A1 "Bazooka" – United States
- Panzerfaust – Germany

FLAMETHROWERS

- M2 Flamethrower – United States

Bazooka

CARRIER PIGEONS

PIGEONS CAN BE TRAINED to return to their home roost from faraway places. They fly undetected by radar and virtually unseen by fast-moving aircraft. All branches of the armed forces—army, navy, coast guard, and marines—used pigeons. The pigeons' home lofts were trailers at air bases or mobile lofts pulled by jeeps.

Soldiers and airmen tucked pigeons into socks, pockets, specially designed slings, or in their shirtfronts on the way into battle. Paratroopers dropped behind enemy lines sent back information about German troop locations and weapon strength. Pigeons were particularly useful in situations when using a radio would have meant discovery by the enemy.

Pigeons carried back to headquarters hastily scribbled messages rolled into canisters attached to their leg or back. The pigeons used in World War II could travel 400 miles in a single flight, at an average of 40 miles an hour. When a pigeon returned to its roost, a bell or buzzer would signal that a message had arrived.

Early in the war, the British Royal Air Force found that one in every seven of its men shot down over the sea owed his life to a message carried by pigeon. When the U.S. joined the war effort, it regularly sent pigeons aboard bombers.

On D-Day, thousands of pigeons were dropped over Normandy in cages with parachutes carrying them to the ground. French civilians were meant to send the pigeons back with detailed information about German troop locations and gun fortifications.

At its height, the Army Signal Corps, which ran the American pigeon service, had 54,000 pigeons. They estimate that 30,000 messages were sent and that an astonishing 96 percent of them were received.

OPERATION FORTITUDE: THE INFLATABLE ARMY

WITH MILLIONS OF TROOPS and thousands of tanks moving to staging areas in England, the Allied command knew that their destinations were very likely to be discovered by German intelligence based in Europe. To counter this, they developed the most extensive deception ever under-  taken in wartime. In effect, they created two fake armies positioned where they wanted the enemy to think the invasions would launch. One FORTITUDE army was a bluff for an invasion into Norway. The other was positioned as if Pas-de-Calais in France were the target.

To create the deception:

- The Allies built inflatable tanks, transport vehicles, and artillery painted with the colors of the real British Third Army. Wooden and rubber war-ships were docked at the harbor in Dover, England.

- The British Royal Air Force allowed German planes to fly somewhat freely over the decoy sites.

- Allied air raid missions were increased over Pas-de-Calais as if to take out enemy defenses to make an Allied landing easier.

- Groups of small boats were sent into the English Channel near the false embarkation sites to create radio signals and other communication as if coming from the decoy sites.

- The Allies slipped false information to their double agents, who trans-mitted the news to Axis intelligence.

CARING FOR THE WOUNDED

THE NATURE OF THE FIGHTING IN

World War II resulted in horrific injuries. Explosive fires on ships caused untold burn injuries and deaths. Bullets, of course, caused many more. In addition, grenades, mortars, mines, and bombs sent shrapnel and fragments racing through anything in their path—necks, legs, stomachs. Seventy-five percent of the penetrating wounds suffered by combat troops in World War II were limb wounds.

Two innovations helped patients immensely: plasma and penicillin. Plasma is the clear part of whole blood and can be dried for easier storage and transport. When mixed with water on the battlefield, it served to help blood clot. Millions of Americans gave blood during the war to supply troops with plasma. Penicillin, used to treat bacterial infections, was invented in 1928 but not mass-produced until the war. Millions of doses were carried into battle.

The surgeon general of the U.S., Norman Kirk, oversaw 535,000 medics, 57,000 nurses, 47,000 physicians, and 2,000 veterinarians. He was the first orthopedic surgeon to serve in the post, and he used his expertise to establish new guidelines for amputation surgeries and rehabilitation for amputees when they got home.

Men on the ground relied on medics, two of whom traveled with each company of soldiers. Seriously injured patients were evacuated to small mobile field hospitals (called MASH units, which stood for Mobile Army Surgical Hospital) and then, if necessary, to one of the 700 overseas local hospitals. More than 600,000 soldiers made it home to be treated in 78 stateside military hospitals.

CLOTHING AND EQUIPMENT ISSUED TO A NEW GI IN 1943

- Goggles
- Field pack (see page 184 for contents)
- Field jacket and hood
- Pile field jacket liner
- Entrenching tool (a folding shovel) and carrying case
- Field trousers
- Rain poncho
- Field cap
- Wool sleeping bag and case
- Pile cap (lined and with earflaps for cold weather)
- Gas mask and carrying case
- Steel helmet (could also be used to hold water to wash or cook in, to dig trenches, or as a weapon)
- High-neck sweater
- Combat service boots

MONTHLY PAY FOR AN AMERICAN GI IN 1940

AMERICAN GIs were more highly paid than other countries' armies. Many, however, would have made more money had they not enlisted.

Master Sergeant and First Sergeant	$138
Technical Sergeant	$114
Staff Sergeant and Technician, Third Grade	$96
Sergeant and Technician, Fourth Grade	$78
Corporal and Technician, Fifth Grade	$66
Private, First Class	$54
Private	$50

WHAT THEY CARRIED— U.S. AIRBORNE DIVISIONS

DROPPED BEHIND ENEMY LINES, paratroopers had to carry everything they might need. Their packs weighed between 70 and 90 pounds. Their parachutes added another 20 pounds.

Standard Parachutist Pack:
- M-1 Garand rifle with 8-round clip
- Cartridge belt with canteen
- Hand grenades
- Parachute and pack
- Fire-resistant headgear and gloves
- Pocket compass
- Machete
- Colt .45-caliber automatic pistol
- Flares
- Message book

In addition to the standard contents, officers also carried plastic high explosives, wire cutters, radio batteries, 48 hours worth of food rations, water, and cooking and washing kits.

Uniforms were designed with many pockets. Into them went:
- Pistols
- Medical kits
- Knives
- Escape/survival kits
- Rope
- Personal items like letters and photographs

Every soldier also had emergency rations that included:
- 4 pieces of chewing gum
- 2 bouillon cubes
- 2 instant coffee packets, 2 sugar cubes, and powdered creamer
- 4 Hershey's chocolate bars
- 1 pack of Charms candy
- Cigarettes
- 1 bottle of water purification tablets

WHAT THEY CARRIED—
U.S. GROUND ASSAULT TROOPS

THE AVERAGE SOLDIER carried 75 pounds of equipment onto the beaches of Normandy. His supplies were new, and so was his uniform. Each soldier was issued many items, including:

- Order of the Day (the instructions from SHAEF outlining who was to land where and when)
- Boxes of matches
- Vomit bags
- Anti-seasickness pills
- 200 franc notes, called invasion currency, which were legal in Occupied France even though they had been printed in the U.S. (about $275 in today's dollars)
- French language guidebook
- Life belt

- Ration heating units (a can with a fuel tablet that, when lit, became a small stove)
- Pocket guide to France
- Raincoat
- Bug repellent powder
- Canteen
- Water purification tablets
- Extra pair of socks
- Candy bars
- Razor blade
- A plastic, waterproof rifle cover
- Cigarettes
- Chewing gum

K RATIONS: FOOD ON THE GO FOR AMERICAN TROOPS

IF SOLDIERS WERE IN ONE PLACE for a day or more, a field kitchen was set up. If not, soldiers received K ration boxes, dipped in wax twice to make them waterproof. In 1944 alone, more than 105 million of these rations were produced for U.S. troops.

The *K* in K ration might have stood for the American physiologist Dr. Ancel Keys, who was tasked with coming up with food for GIs that had sufficient calories, did not have to be refrigerated, and could fit in a uniform pocket. Other records suggest that, like the *D* in D-Day, *K* didn't stand for a specific word; it might have been chosen because it sounds different from other letters.

Each K ration included three boxed meals:

BREAKFAST
Canned ham and eggs or veal loaf, a cereal bar, a fruit bar, crackers, powdered coffee, sugar cubes, water purification tablets, four cigarettes, and chewing gum, plus a can opener and a wooden spoon.

DINNER (THE MIDDAY MEAL)
Canned processed cheese and/or ham, crackers, a candy bar, a powdered juice drink, granulated sugar, salt tablets, four cigarettes, matches, chewing gum, plus a can opener and a wooden spoon.

SUPPER
One main course of canned pork luncheon meat with carrots and apples, or chicken pâté, or beef and pork loaf, or sausages as well as crackers, a bouillon soup powder packet, a chocolate bar, powdered coffee, granulated sugar, four cigarettes, chewing gum, and a packet of toilet paper tissues, plus a can opener and a wooden spoon.

NUMBERS TELL PART OF THE STORY

D-DAY AT A GLANCE

Allied troops landed	156,000*
First soldier to land from the sea	Sergeant Harvey S. Olson, U.S. 4th Cavalry†
Ships and landing craft	5,000
Planes	11,000
Vehicles	30,000
Parachutists	13,000
Bombs dropped over coastal Normandy	13,000
Allied killed, wounded, missing, or captured	12,000

WORLD WAR II AT A GLANCE

How long the war lasted	2,174 days
Countries involved in World War II	61
Americans who served	16.1 million
United Kingdom citizens who served	5.9 million
Canadians who served	1.1 million
People worldwide who served	1.9 billion
Average time each U.S. serviceman spent overseas	16 months
Bombs dropped by Allies	3.4 million tons
Airplanes that the U.S. 8th Air Force shot down	6,098
Americans missing or captured at the end of the war	75,000
American pilots believed killed behind enemy lines	14,000
Estimated number of GIs buried in Europe	25,000
U.S. military dead	416,800
U.S. civilian dead	1,700‡
U.S. soldiers wounded	671,278

Philippine military dead	57,000
Philippine civilian dead	500,000–1,000,000[§]
U.K. military dead	383,600
U.K. civilian dead	67,100
U.K. soldiers wounded	326,000
Canadian military dead	23,000
Canadian soldiers wounded	54,000
Soviet military dead	8.8–10.7 million
Soviet civilian dead	13–15 million
Soviet soldiers wounded	14,915,517
German military dead	5,533,000
German civilian dead	1,067,000–3,267,000
German soldiers wounded	6,035,000
European Jews killed during the Holocaust	6 million
Japanese dead in Hiroshima bombing	90,000–120,000[‖]
Japanese dead in Nagasaki bombing	60,000–80,000[‖]
Deaths worldwide	72 million[#]

*From the U.S., U.K., Canada, Free France, and Norway.

[†]Olson survived D-Day and the war.

[‡]1,500 American citizens were living in Japan at the time of the declaration of war. They died in internment camps. About 180 U.S. citizens were living in Germany and also died in captivity. At Pearl Harbor, 68 civilians died.

[§]The Philippines, which was controlled by the U.S. at the outbreak of war, was taken by the Japanese. The number of civilian deaths is the result of military action (about 100,000) and famine and disease (400,000–900,000).

[‖]Many more died later of diseases caused by radiation poisoning.

[#]27,600 every day of the war, 1,150 every hour, or 19 every minute.

OPERATION OVERLORD TIMELINE

DECEMBER 1943

Dwight D. Eisenhower is named supreme commander of Operation OVERLORD, the planned Allied invasion of north-western Europe.

FEBRUARY 1944

Adolf Hitler puts Erwin Rommel in charge of defending the 2,400-mile Atlantic Wall, the western coasts of France, Belgium, the Netherlands, Denmark, and Norway.

MAY 5, 1944

Eisenhower, the Allied commanders and staff, and the king of England meet at St. Paul's School in London to finalize plans for the invasion.

JUNE 1944

Minesweepers begin to clear a 15-mile-wide path south from England to Normandy. On D-Day they continue to sweep paths to the beaches for landing craft and artillery support ships.

JUNE 3–4, 1944

Bad weather arrives and is forecast for June 5, the day Eisenhower had chosen for D-Day. He calls for a 24-hour delay.

JUNE 5, 1944
4 A.M.

Eisenhower gives the go-ahead for a June 6 assault that will involve 132,700 troops, 23,400 paratroopers, and 6,485 ships and landing craft.

6 A.M.–10 P.M.

Convoys of troop ships with their warship escorts leave English ports, gather at the Isle of Wight, and turn south toward Normandy beaches.

10 P.M.

11,000 aircraft mobilize to provide cover for the invasion.

D-DAY: JUNE 6, 1944
Midnight

The first airborne troops land.

1 A.M.

Landing craft begin to be lowered into the water.

1:30 A.M.

Rommel's army groups are placed on alert following intelligence that Allied paratroopers have landed.

2 A.M.

The first bombers, the

8th U.S. Air Force, take off from airfields in England to attack targets near the beaches. By 5:30 A.M., 1,198 aircraft are headed for the coast and another 163 for the city of Caen.

2:29 A.M.
Flagship U.S.S. *Bayfield* drops anchor 11.5 miles off Utah Beach.

2:45–4:15 A.M.
Troops bound for the beaches climb down from transport ships into landing craft.

2:51 A.M.
Flagship U.S.S. *Ancon* drops anchor 11 miles off Omaha Beach.

3 A.M.
Gliders towed by C-47s begin to reinforce paratroops.

5:30 A.M.–7 A.M.
Rocket launcher barges approach the beaches to clear enemy guns. 20,000 rockets will be launched at the British and Canadian beaches, 18,000 at the American beaches.

5:35 A.M.
German shore batteries open fire.

5:58 A.M.
Sunrise over Normandy beaches.

6:20 A.M.
The amphibious invasion begins as Allied landing craft approach the beaches.

6:30 A.M.
American troops land on Utah and Omaha Beaches.

7:25 A.M.
British troops land on Sword and Gold Beaches.

7:30 A.M.
Canadian troops land on Juno Beach.

10 A.M.
The village of Vierville falls to the Allies.

10:45 A.M.
Utah Beach is secure.

1 P.M.
Troops begin to secure Omaha Beach.

4 P.M.
Men from 3rd Canadian Division reach three miles inland.

7 P.M.
Division commander General Clarence R. Heubner sets up a command post on Omaha Beach.

9:15 P.M.
An airstrip opens alongside Utah Beach, the first of 214 airstrips U.S. troops will build in the following 11 months to allow supplies and troops to land quickly.

DAY'S END

156,000 troops had parachuted, glided, or stormed the beaches. Reinforcements continued to arrive. The Allies had captured territory and defeated the enemy in an area 10 miles deep and 60 miles wide. The Allies will continue to fight their way across western Europe.

GLOSSARY

AFTERDECK–the deck area of a ship behind the bridge

ANGLO–an English or British person

AUTOCRACY–a government in which one person or group possesses unlimited power

BATTALION–an army group usually of three or more companies

BATTERY–an artillery grouping with six or more guns

BATTLE DRESS–uniform worn in combat

BIFF–to punch or strike a blow

BILGE PUMP–a pump to remove water or other fluid from a boat

BIVOUAC–an improvised shelter (noun); to sleep outside without proper tents (verb)

BLINKERED–narrow-minded

BOW–the front end of a ship

BREECH–the rear part of a gun's barrel into which ammunition is placed to be fired

BRIGADIER–senior officer in the army or marines who usually commands a brigade

CASEMATE–a fortified position, chamber, or armored enclosure from which guns can be fired

CAUSEWAY–a raised road above wet ground or water

CLOUD CEILING–the height of the lowest clouds over ground or water

CORP–an army group usually of two or more divisions

COXSWAIN–the person who steers the boat or ship

CRICKET–a small metal toy used as a signaling device because it makes a sharp click or snap when pressed

DISPERSION–the spreading out or separating of troops

E-BOAT–German fast-attack surface boat

EBB TIDE–tide that is moving out to sea

ENTRENCH–to dig in

ESCARPMENT–a cliff or slope

FASCIST–a form of government in which a dictator and the dictator's political party have complete power over a country

FATHOM—a unit of length equal to six feet, usually used to measure the depth of water

FENS—low land that is covered wholly or in part by water

FLANK—area to the left or right of a formation

FLARE—device used to give brief, bright light

FORECASTLE—the forward part of a ship

FOULED—entangled in weeds or other debris

FOUR-STAR FLAG—a rectangular flag with four white stars on a solid red background, signifying a U.S. Army four-star general

FREEBOARD—the distance between the waterline and the deck of a boat or ship

FUSELAGE—the main body of an aircraft designed to hold passengers or cargo

GAS—a chemical weapon in the form of a gas used to blind, choke, or kill such as mustard bombs or gas artillery shells

GODSPEED—an exclamation of good wishes as someone leaves

GROUSE—birds, similar to chickens, that are hunted for food and sport

GUNWALE—the top edge of the side of a boat

HOWITZER—a short cannon

INSIGNIA—a decorative symbol used to designate a unit, rank, or specialist qualification

LCI—"landing craft, infantry," amphibious assault ship used to unload large numbers of troops directly onto beaches

LCT—"landing craft, tank," an amphibious assault ship for landing tanks onto beaches

LODGEMENT—an area that, when captured, makes further landing of troops and matériel possible

LOGISTICS—the coordination of the supply and resupply of all items troops need in battle, such as ammunition, equipment, food and water, medical supplies, spare parts, and replacement men

LST—"landing ship, tank," a ship designed to support amphibious craft and transport troops, cargo, and armored vehicles

LUFTWAFFE—the German air force

MASTICATE—chew

MATÉRIEL—military equipment and supplies

MECHANIZED—equipped with armored personnel carriers or infantry fighting vehicles

MERCHANT MARINE—fleet of civilian-owned vessels used to help the navy transport troops and supplies

MESS—short for "mess hall," the building where people in the armed services eat their meals

MONITOR—a small boat with a shallow draft for coastal bombardment

MORTAR—a front-loading cannon

OSCILLOSCOPE—a machine used to detect radar

PARADE (TO)—to assemble at a designated time and place

PARADE DRILL—an assembly in formation

PAYLOAD—the weapons and munitions carried by an aircraft; the type of munition delivered by a missile

PERSONNEL MINE—a small mine intended to hurt or kill humans

PILLBOX—a small, low concrete fortification that houses machine guns and antitank weapons

PORT—the left side of an aircraft, boat, or ship looking forward

RISER—the strap that connects a parachute harness with the lines of the parachute canopy

SABOTEUR—a civilian or enemy agent who carries out destructive or obstructive actions to hinder a nation's war effort

SAPPER—a military demolitions specialist

SCYTHE—a hand tool for mowing grass or cutting crops

SPOILING ATTACK—an attack mounted on an advancing enemy in order to disrupt its activities

STARBOARD—the right side of an aircraft, boat, or ship looking forward

STERN—the rear part of a ship

STEVEDORE—a skilled laborer who loads and off-loads ships at port

SYRETTE—a device similar to a syringe containing one dose of medicine, designed to be carried by soldiers to treat themselves

THIRD REICH—the name Hitler used for his empire

TOMMY GUN—Thompson submachine gun

TRACER—a bullet designed to ignite on firing and burn in flight so one can see where the shot went

TRUNK CABLE—a circuit that connects two telephone exchanges

U-BOAT—German military submarine

ULTRA—the Allied Intelligence project whose members specialized in decrypting intercepted German messages using electrical cipher machines

WADDING—soft cotton used to hold explosives in place within a gun barrel

WEHRMACHT—the unified armed forces of Germany from 1939 to 1945 made up of the Heer (army), Kriegsmarine (navy), and Luftwaffe (air force)

PLACES TO VISIT

NATIONAL WORLD WAR II MEMORIAL

17th Street SW
Washington, D.C.
nps.gov/nwwm

The open-air memorial stands at one end of the reflecting pool on the Mall in Washington, D.C., between the Washington Monument and the Lincoln Memorial. It consists of an Atlantic pavilion at one side and a Pacific pavilion at the other, honoring the two theaters of battle. Fifty-six pillars around a fountain name the 48 states that were in the union in 1945, plus the District of Columbia, the territories of Hawaii and Alaska, Guam, the Philippines, Puerto Rico, American Samoa, and the U.S. Virgin Islands. The Memorial is operated by the National Park Service, whose park rangers give tours and are available on-site to answer questions.

There are three databases associated with the memorial: of those buried overseas in military cemeteries, of those missing in action, and of those killed in action.

NATIONAL WORLD WAR II MUSEUM

945 Magazine Street
New Orleans, LA
nationalww2museum.org

This is the country's official World War II museum. Through photographs and artifacts, it tells the story of the many Americans who fought, the various places they struggled, and the scores of people at home who supported them. You can see full-scale replicas of the boats that carried soldiers to the beaches on D-Day as well as a real C-47, Spitfire planes, and a Sherman tank. Weapons, clothing, K rations, and medical kits are also on display.

CANADIAN WAR MUSEUM

1 Vimy Place
Ottawa, Canada
warmuseum.ca

Artifacts—including aircraft, tanks, other vehicles, and ammunitions—bring to life personal stories, photographs, and interactive exhibits to describe the history of Canadians at war and at home during war years. The dramatic modern building includes a memorial hall and gallery.

IMPERIAL WAR MUSEUM, LONDON

Lambeth Road
London, England
iwm.org.uk

Five museums in England, including the ship H.M.S. *Belfast* and the Winston Churchill War Rooms, explore England's military history. The permanent exhibits focus on military heroes, the Holocaust, England's secret war of covert operations, and family life in London during World War II.

UNITED STATES HOLOCAUST MEMORIAL MUSEUM

100 Raoul Wallenberg Place SW
Washington, D.C.
ushmm.org

The museum is a living memorial to the Holocaust intended to educate people about the dangers of hatred and persecution. Tailored guides for students and families help make a visit to this museum impactful.

FOR MORE INFORMATION

BOOKS:

Adams, Simon. *Eyewitness World War II*. New York: DK Publishing Inc, 2004.

Allen, Thomas. *Remember Pearl Harbor: American and Japanese Survivors Tell Their Stories*. Washington, D.C.: National Geographic, 2001.

Ambrose, Stephen E. *The Good Fight: How World War II Was Won*. New York: Atheneum Books for Young Readers, 2001.

Bliven, Bruce, Jr. *The Story of D-Day: June 6, 1944*. New York: Random House, 1956, 1994.

Bowden, Mark. *Our Finest Day: D-Day: June 4, 1944*. San Francisco: Chronicle Books, 2002.

Drez, Ronald J. *Remember D-Day: The Plan, the Invasion, Survivor Stories*. Washington, D.C.: National Geographic, 2004.

Evans, A. A., and David Gibbons. *The Illustrated Timeline of World War II*. New York: Rosen Publishing Group, 2012.

Frank, Anne. *The Diary of a Young Girl*. New York: Doubleday, 1947, 2001.

Hynson, Colin. *World War II: A Primary Source History*. Pleasantville, NY: Gareth Stevens, Inc., 2006.

Martin, Chris. *World War II Book of Lists*. Gloucestershire, U.K.: The History Press, 2011.

Nicholson, Dorinda. *Remember World War II: Kids Who Survived Tell Their Stories*. Washington, D.C.: National Geographic, 2005.

Platt, Richard. *D-Day Landings: The Story of the Allied Invasion*. New York: DK Publishing, 2004.

Tanaka, Shelley. *D-Day: They Fought to Free Europe from Hitler's Tyranny*. New York: Hyperion Books for Children, 2003.

Whitmarsh, Andrew. *D-Day in Photographs*. Stroud, Gloucestershire, England: The History Press, 2009.

WEB SITES:

British Broadcasting Corporation
bbc.co.uk/schools/primaryhistory/world_war2/

Canadian War Museum
warmuseum.ca

Imperial War Museum (UK)
iwm.org.uk

National World War II Museum (US)
nationalww2museum.org

Public Broadcasting Service
pbs.org/wgbh/amex/dday/

Smithsonian Museum
si.edu (search for World War II or D-Day)

BIBLIOGRAPHY

THIS BOOK IS A VERSION of an adult book called *The Guns at Last Light*, part of my Liberation Trilogy. Below are several titles from the complete bibliography for the trilogy. A complete list, with comments, is available at liberationtrilogy.com/books/wwii-resources.

For a big-picture understanding of the global war, I recommend *A World at Arms* by Gerhard L. Weinberg, *Inferno: The World at War, 1939–1945* by Max Hastings, *The Second World War* by Antony Beevor, *A War to Be Won* by Williamson Murray and Allan R. Millett, *The Struggle for Europe* by Chester Wilmot, and *Why the Allies Won* by Richard Overy.

Perhaps the most vivid and tactile account of the war can be found at the National World War II Museum in New Orleans. Over the past decade, the museum has vastly expanded its artifacts, pavilions, and archival holdings; it now offers a thorough, compelling experience about the war's origins, campaigns, personalities, and consequences. For more information, visit the Web site at nationalww2museum.org.

In western Europe, for the Normandy invasion, noteworthy works include *D-Day* by Antony Beevor, *Decision in Normandy* by Carlo D'Este, *Six Armies in Normandy* by John Keegan, *Normandy* by Olivier Wieviorka, *Pegasus Bridge* by Stephen E. Ambrose, and *Omaha Beach* and *Utah Beach* by Joseph Balkoski.

IMAGE CREDITS

Permission to use the following images is gratefully acknowledged:

Alamy: 43, 49 (bottom), 86 (top), 93, 96, 115, 132, 153

Associated Press: 24, 40, 45, 78, 84

Corbis: xxii (top), 29 (top), 29 (bottom), 34, 37, 122

Gene Thorp: 10, 56–57

Library of Congress: x, 3, 11, 17, 20, 71, 172, 174, 175, 185

Magnum: 118, 119

Bridgeman Art Library: 3, 8, 9, 13, 33, 73, 77, 82, 90, 98, 99, 100, 101, 106, 110, 111, 114, 126, 128, 141, 142, 144, 151, 155, 157, 158 (top), 158 (bottom), 159, 160 (top), 163 (top), 163 (bottom), 164, 169, 170, 171, 178, 180

Imperial War Museum: 2, 12, 22, 23, 26, 28, 31, 32, 35, 41, 42, 47, 80, 135

Mary Evans Picture Library: xxii (bottom), 6, 14, 18, 25, 38, 49 (top), 52 (bottom), 52 (top), 58, 62, 67, 69, 85, 86 (bottom), 87, 89, 124, 127, 129, 130, 134, 136, 139, 146, 148, 161, 165, 176, 179, 182

Shutterstock: 194

U.S. National Archives and Records Administration: endpapers, xx–xxi, 4, 5, 7, 50–51, 55, 61, 65, 95, 102, 105, 107, 109, 113, 121, 138, 154, 160, 162, 166, 173, 181

INDEX

GI Bill, 165

GIs, American, 25–29
  clothing and equipment for, 182
  combat loads carried by, 39–40, 42,
    49, 60–61, 183, 184
  French handbooks for, 46–47
  gathering in British Isles, 25–26,
    34–35
  ideals and inner beliefs of, 28–29
  letter writing of, 61–62
  monthly pay of, 182
  ships boarded by, 42–43, 52
  typical, 26–27
  see also Paratroopers

Glide bombs, 90

Gliders and glidermen, 24, 45, 60, 61, 62,
  67, 69, 71–189, 72, 75, 77, 78, 149
  Horsa gliders ("Flying Morgues"), 69,
    81–82
  in offensive for bridges over Orne and
    at Caen, 81–83, 135, 137
  Waco gliders, 71–72, 73

Gold Beach, 65, 96, 110, 131–33, 150, 189

Great Britain, viii–xix, xii, xiii, 4–6, 187
  airborne forces of, 79–84. See also
    Gliders and glidermen
  casualty figures for, 20–21, 169, 187
  soldiers from, at Gold, Juno, and
    Sword beaches, 131–35, 136, 137, 189

H

Hand grenades, 178

Hemingway, Ernest, xvii, 97, 103

Heubner, Clarence R., 189

Hitler, Adolf, xii, xiii, xv, xvii, 4, 5, 13,
  18, 79, 90, 139, 140, 143–44, 147, 148,
  156, 188

Holocaust, viii, 166, 187

Horsa gliders ("Flying Morgues"), 69,
  81–83

Howard, John, xvii, 81, 82, 137

I

Italy, xi, xii, xiii, xiv, 4, 5, 60, 62, 90

J

Jamming operations, 88, 89–90

Japan, xi, xiii, xv, 4, 162, 163, 172, 187

Jarrell, Randall, xvii, 26

Jews, mass murder of, xiii, 166, 187

Jodl, Alfred, xvii, 160

Juno Beach, 65, 96, 131–33, 135–38, 150,
  189

K

Keegan, John, xvii, 114

Keitel, Wilhelm, 160

K rations, 185

Krause, Edward C. "Cannonball," xvii,
  76, 77

L

LCIs (landing craft, infantry), 55, 95,
  118, 119

LCTs (landing craft, tank), 12, 55–58, 65,
  89, 114, 131

Leigh-Mallory, Trafford, xvii, xxii, 44, 45,
  46, 48, 63, 78

Liebling, A. J., xvii, 97

London, V-E Day in, 162–63

LSTs (landing ship tank, or tank landing
  ship), 12, 33, 42–43, 55, 155
  torpedoed off coast of England, 22–24

Luftwaffe, xii, 90, 142–43

M

MacArthur, Douglas, 163

Machine guns, light, 178

Marshall, George, xvii, 24, 64, 163, 167

Matériel, 30–33
  camouflage of, 36–37
  supplied by Americans, 164–65
  waterproofing of, 39

McCloughry, E. J. Kingston, xvii, 46

Medical staff and supplies, 26, 33–34,
  181

Merderet River, 70, 74, 75–76

Merville battery, 83–84

Millin, Bill, xvii, 135, 137

Mine detectors, 131

Minesweepers, 54, 85, 95–96, 105, 188

Montgomery, Bernard L., xvii, xxii, 9, 20,
  44, 46, 48, 59
  in D-Day planning, 9–15, 16–17

Moon, Don P., xvii, 105–6, 124

Moorehead, Alan, xvii, 35, 53, 152

We French workers warn you...
defeat means slavery, starvation, death

REMEMBER DEC. 7th!

BUY WAR BONDS